Emotionally Healthy
Relationships

WORKBOOK

The Emotionally Healthy Discipleship Course

by Peter and Geri Scazzero

A proven strategy that moves people from shallow discipleship to deep transformation in Christ.

PART 1

Introducing people to a transformative spirituality with God.

Emotionally Healthy Spirituality
- Eight-session DVD video study
- Workbook plus Streaming Video access
- Book
- Day by Day devotional

PART 2

Practical skills to launch people into a transformative spirituality with others.

Emotionally Healthy Relationships
- Eight-session DVD video study
- Workbook plus Streaming Video access
- Day by Day devotional

ALSO BY PETER SCAZZERO

The Emotionally Healthy Leader
The Emotionally Healthy Woman (with Geri Scazzero)
Emotionally Healthy Discipleship

emotionally
HEALTHY DISCIPLESHIP

ZONDERVAN®

Emotionally Healthy
Relationships

DISCIPLESHIP *that* DEEPLY CHANGES
YOUR RELATIONSHIP *with* OTHERS

UPDATED EDITION

WORKBOOK

EIGHT SESSIONS

Peter and Geri Scazzero

HarperChristian Resources

Emotionally Healthy Relationships Workbook Updated Edition
Copyright © 2017, 2021 by Peter and Geri Scazzero

Requests for information should be addressed to:
HarperChristian Resources, *3900 Sparks Dr. SE, Grand Rapids, Michigan 49546*

ISBN: 978-0-310-14567-7 (softcover)
ISBN: 978-0-310-14568-4 (ebook)

Cover image: ©Brian Kinney/www.123RF.com
Interior design: Kait Lamphere

First Printing November 2021 / Printed in the United States of America

Contents

Acknowledgments

We want to thank Ron Vogt for teaching us our first Emotionally Healthy Relationships Skill in January 1996 and providing the seed God would use to radically change our lives and marriage.

Lori Gordon, the creator of the Pairs Foundation (www.pairs.com), demonstrated for us the power of putting skills together to transform relationships through her 120-hour master course. We are deeply indebted to her pioneering work in the field of relationship education.

We are also thankful for the brilliant and pioneering work of Virginia Satir, who originally developed the Community Temperature Reading. Many thanks to the Virginia Satir Global Network (www.satirglobal.org) for the permission to make this tool widely known to the church world.

We are deeply grateful to Carol and Peter Shreck (Pete's professors at Eastern University) for their painful, life-changing assignment that Pete interview every living member of his family in a yearlong project to genogram his family.

Thanks to Pat Ennis at Third Option (www.thethirdoption.com) for the development of the Clarify Expectations skill and the permission for our use of it.

We wish also to thank the New Life Fellowship Church family, along with the many pastors and leaders from around the world with whom we have been piloting and revising these skills over the past twenty-one years. Your honest feedback has given each of these skills precision, depth, and cultural nuancing.

Finally, thank you to John Raymond, TJ Rathbun, Greg Clouse, and the Zondervan team for kindly and widely shepherding this project to completion.

Introduction

Have you ever wondered why we recycle the same problems in the church year after year? Broken relationships, unresolved conflicts, inability to speak the truth, pretending things are fine because we're concerned about being nice. Week after week we hear sermons about loving better, but little changes in people's lives.

It's been rightly said that 85 percent of Christians are stuck, stagnant in their spiritual lives. We were among that number, especially as it related to how to grow practically into more loving people. We discovered that a commitment to a personal relationship with Jesus and to spiritual disciplines does not automatically equip us to love like Jesus. That requires intentional discipleship.

To address this need we developed the *Emotionally Healthy Discipleship Course: Part 1* and *Part 2* over a twenty-one year period. While *Part 1: Emotionally Healthy Spirituality* focuses on moving us to a transformative relationship with God, *Emotionally Healthy Relationships, Part 2*, equips us with skills to radically transform our relationships with others. It is possible to begin with Part 1 or Part 2 since they function as one, separable Course.

the emotionally healthy
DISCIPLESHIP COURSE

PART 1

PART 2

EMOTIONALLY HEALTHY SPIRITUALITY
1. The Problem of Emotionally Unhealthy Spirituality
2. Know Yourself that You May Know God
3. Going Back to Go Forward
4. Journey through the Wall
5. Enlarge Your Soul through Grief and Loss
6. Discover the Rhythms of the Daily Office and Sabbath
7. Grow into an Emotionally Mature Adult
8. Go the Next Step to Develop a Rule of Life

EMOTIONALLY HEALTHY RELATIONSHIPS
1. Take Your Community Temperature Reading
2. Stop Mind Reading & Clarify Expectations
3. Genogram Your Family
4. Explore the Iceberg
5. Listen Incarnationally
6. Climb the Ladder of Integrity
7. Fight Cleanly
8. Develop a Rule of Life to Implement Your New Skills

We spend a lot of money to learn, and become competent in, our careers, but few of us have learned the skills or gained the competency to love well. Most discipleship approaches do not include the necessary tools to mature us as followers of Jesus Christ who love God, ourselves, and others well.

The *Emotionally Healthy Relationship Course* (or the *EH Relationships Course*) will train you in eight skills for building a healthy church, or community, where our love for one another is so distinct that the world will know Jesus is truly alive today. Our hope and prayer is that you will learn these skills so well that they become second nature to you and that you carry them into your church, workplace, family, school, and neighborhood.

This workbook is part of a larger course that includes two companion resources—the *EH Relationships Course* video and the *Emotionally Healthy Relationships Day by Day* devotional. On the video, we explain and model each of the eight skills before you actually practice them yourself during the sessions. The *Emotionally Healthy Relationships Day by Day* devotional is designed to deepen your personal, firsthand relationship with Jesus by incorporating, stillness, silence and Scripture into your daily life rhythms. Why? Loving God and loving people, as Jesus said, are inseparable.

On the last page of the workbook, you will find a checklist to keep you on track as you move through the course. Fill it out along the way and, when completed, go to emotionally-healthy.org to receive your certificate of completion.

Don't worry if the skills feel a bit awkward at first. That is to be expected as you step into a wonderfully, new way of relating to God, yourself, and others.

How to Use This Workbook

Before Session 1

- Purchase *Emotionally Healthy Relationships Day by Day* and this workbook.
- Read the introduction to Session 1 in the workbook.
- Watch the seven-minute video that introduces how to use *Emotionally Healthy Relationships Day by Day* at www.emotionallyhealthy.org/vault or YouTube.

Throughout the Study

The key to receive the impact of this workbook is what comes around it. Each week you will be asked to do a Pre-Session Reading from the *Emotionally Healthy Relationships Workbook* before the Session, engage the *Emotionally Healthy Relationships Workbook* during the session, and read the corresponding *Emotionally Healthy Relationships Day by Day* devotionals after the Session. The chart on the next page gives you a visual roadmap for what to do each week.

You will also find, at the end of each session in this workbook, a "Between-Sessions Personal Study" section. This is based on questions from the Daily Offices found in the *Emotionally Healthy Relationships Day by Day* devotional.

The Leader's Guide in the back of this workbook provides extremely helpful information to supplement the studies. We encourage you to avail yourselves of this valuable material. Additional free resources for this Course can be found at www.emotionallyhealthy.org/vault.

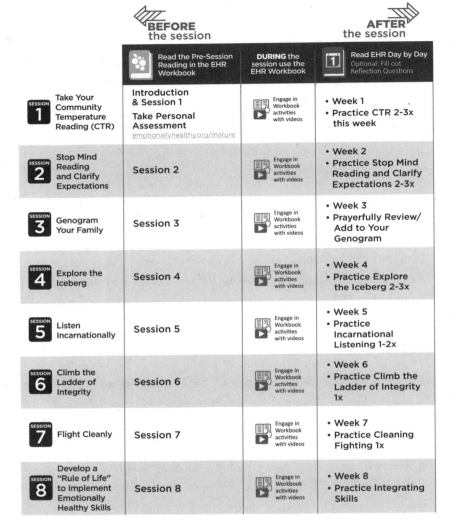

		BEFORE the session		AFTER the session
		Read the Pre-Session Reading in the EHR Workbook	DURING the session use the EHR Workbook	Read EHR Day by Day Optional: Fill out Reflection Questions
SESSION 1	Take Your Community Temperature Reading (CTR)	Introduction & Session 1 Take Personal Assessment emotionallyhealthy.org/mature	Engage in Workbook activities with videos	• Week 1 • Practice CTR 2-3x this week
SESSION 2	Stop Mind Reading and Clarify Expectations	Session 2	Engage in Workbook activities with videos	• Week 2 • Practice Stop Mind Reading and Clarify Expectations 2-3x
SESSION 3	Genogram Your Family	Session 3	Engage in Workbook activities with videos	• Week 3 • Prayerfully Review/ Add to Your Genogram
SESSION 4	Explore the Iceberg	Session 4	Engage in Workbook activities with videos	• Week 4 • Practice Explore the Iceberg 2-3x
SESSION 5	Listen Incarnationally	Session 5	Engage in Workbook activities with videos	• Week 5 • Practice Incarnational Listening 1-2x
SESSION 6	Climb the Ladder of Integrity	Session 6	Engage in Workbook activities with videos	• Week 6 • Practice Climb the Ladder of Integrity 1x
SESSION 7	Flight Cleanly	Session 7	Engage in Workbook activities with videos	• Week 7 • Practice Cleaning Fighting 1x
SESSION 8	Develop a "Rule of Life" to Implement Emotionally Healthy Skills	Session 8	Engage in Workbook activities with videos	• Week 8 • Practice Integrating Skills

IMPORTANT NOTE ON THE VIDEOS

The video presentations for each Session are available FREE through streaming access for you to review each week. Simply use the code found on the inside front cover of the Workbook.

You an also access them wherever books/DVD's are sold, or by digital video through sites such as amazon.com, vimeo.com, and christianbook.com.

Guidelines for the Group

Be Prepared

To get the most out of your time together, we ask that you do the pre-session readings. Please also bring your workbook and the *EH Relationships Day by Day* book with you to each meeting.

Speak for Yourself

We encourage you to share and use "I" statements. We are only experts on ourselves. For example: Instead of saying, "Everyone is busy," say, "I am busy." Instead of saying, "We all struggle with forgiving," say, "I struggle with forgiving."

Respect Others

Be brief in your sharing, remaining mindful that there are time limitations and others may want to share.

No Fixing, Saving, No Setting Other People Straight

Respect people's journeys and trust the Holy Spirit inside of them to lead them into all truth—in his timing. Resist the temptation to offer quick advice as people share in the group.

Turn to Wonder

If you feel judgmental or defensive when someone else is sharing, ask yourself: *I wonder what brought him/her to this belief? I wonder what he/she is feeling right now? I wonder what my reaction teaches me about myself?*

Trust and Learn from Silence

It is okay to have silence between responses as the group shares, giving members the opportunity to reflect. Remember, there is no pressure to share.

Observe Confidentiality

In order to create an environment that is safe for open and honest participation, anything someone shares within the group should not be repeated outside of the group. However, feel free to share your own story and personal growth.

Punctuality

Resolve to arrive on time.

Take Your Community Temperature Reading (CTR)

Session One

THE EMOTIONALLY HEALTHY DISCIPLESHIP PERSONAL ASSESSMENT

What comes to mind when you think of an emotionally healthy disciple? How would you describe that person? While this book will expound on many different facets, the foundational definition of an emotionally healthy disciple is both simpler and more multifaceted than you might expect:

An emotionally healthy disciple slows down to be *with Jesus*, goes beneath the surface of their life to be deeply transformed *by Jesus*, and offers their life as a gift to the world *for Jesus*.

An emotionally healthy disciple refers to a person who rejects busyness and hurry in order to reorient their entire life around their personal relationship *with Jesus*, developing rhythms, setting limits, and following him wherever he leads. At the same time, they intentionally open the depths of their interior life—their history, their disorientations, their areas of brokenness, and their relationships—to be changed *by Jesus*. And they are deeply aware how everything they have and all they are is a gift. So they carry a profound awareness of stewarding their talents as a gift to bless the world *for Jesus*.

The following assessment is designed to help you get a picture of where you're at right now with your own spiritual and emotional maturity. It will help you get a sense of whether your discipleship has touched the emotional components of your life, and if so, how much. It will challenge you to consider whether you are an emotional infant, child, adolescent, or adult. Each of these stages of emotional maturity is described at the end of the chapter.

Even if some of the questions make you feel uneasy or uncomfortable, I invite you to answer with honesty and vulnerability. Be as open as possible before God, who loves you right where you are. Remember, the assessment will reveal nothing about you that is news to him. You may want to take a moment to pray, inviting God to guide your responses.

Next to each statement below through page 31, circle the number that best describes your response.

Emotional/Spiritual Health Inventory

Please answer these questions as honestly as possible.
Use the scoring method as indicated.

Not very true / Sometimes true / Mostly true / Very true

Mark 1. Be Before You Do

1. I spend sufficient time alone with God to sustain my work for God so that I live out of a cup that overflows (Mark 1:35; Luke 6:12). 1 2 3 4

2. It is easy for me to identify what I am feeling inside (Luke 19:41–44; John 11:33–35). 1 2 3 4

3. When I become anxious or feel like I have too much to do in too little time, I stop and slow down to be with God and myself as a way to recenter (Luke 4:42; Luke 10:38–42). 1 2 3 4

4. I set apart a twenty-four-hour period each week for Sabbath-keeping—to stop, to rest, to delight, and to contemplate God (Exodus 20:8–11). 1 2 3 4

5. People close to me would describe me as content, non-defensive, and free from the approval or disapproval of others (Philippians 4:11–12; John 5:44). 1 2 3 4

6. I regularly spend time in solitude and silence. This enables me to be still and undistracted in God's presence (Habakkuk 2:1–4; Psalm 46:10). 1 2 3 4

Mark 1 Total _____

Mark 2. Follow the Crucified, Not the Americanized, Jesus

1. I have rejected the world's definition of success (e.g., bigger is better, be popular, attain earthly security) to become the person God has called me to become and to do what God has called me to do (John 4:34; Mark 14:35–39). 1 2 3 4

2. I rarely change the way I act so others will think highly of me or to assure a particular outcome (Matthew 6:1–2; Galatians 1:10). 1 2 3 4

3. I take a lot of time to carefully discern when my plans and ambitions are legitimately for the glory of God and when they cross the line into my own desire for greatness (Jeremiah 45:5; Mark 10:42–45). 1 2 3 4

4. Listening to Jesus and surrendering my will to his will is more important than any other project, program, or cause (Matthew 17:5; John 16:13). 1 2 3 4

5. People close to me would describe me as patient and calm during failures, disappointments, and setbacks (Isaiah 30:15; John 18:10–11). 1 2 3 4

Mark 2 Total _____

Mark 3. Embrace God's Gift of Limits

1. I've never been accused of "trying to do it all" or of biting off more than I could chew (Matthew 4:1–11).   1 2 3 4

2. I am regularly able to say no to requests and opportunities rather than risk overextending myself (Mark 6:30–32).   1 2 3 4

3. I recognize the different situations where my unique, God-given personality can be either a help or a hindrance in responding appropriately (Psalm 139; Romans 12:3).   1 2 3 4

4. It's easy for me to distinguish the difference between when to help carry someone else's burden and when to let it go so they can carry their own burden (Galatians 6:2, 5).   1 2 3 4

5. I have a good sense of my emotional, relational, physical, and spiritual capacities, intentionally pulling back to rest and replenish (Mark 1:21–39).   1 2 3 4

6. Those close to me would say that I am good at balancing family, rest, work, and play in a biblical way (Exodus 20:8).   1 2 3 4

Mark 3 Total _____

Mark 4. Discover the Hidden Treasures Buried in Grief and Loss

1. I openly admit my losses and disappointments (Psalm 3, 5).   1 2 3 4

2. When I go through a disappointment or a loss, I reflect on how I'm feeling rather than pretend that nothing is wrong (2 Samuel 1:4, 17–27; Psalm 51:1–17).   1 2 3 4

3. I take time to grieve my losses as David and Jesus did (Psalm 69; Matthew 26:39; John 11:35; 12:27).   1 2 3 4

4. People who are in great pain and sorrow tend to seek me out because it's clear to them that I am in touch with the losses and sorrows in my own life (2 Corinthians 1:3–7).   1 2 3 4

5. I am able to cry and experience depression or sadness, explore the reasons behind it, and allow God to work in me through it (Psalm 42; Matthew 26:36–46).   1 2 3 4

Mark 4 Total _____

	Not very true	Sometimes true	Mostly true	Very true

Mark 5. Make Love the Measure of Spiritual Maturity

1. I am regularly able to enter into the experiences and feelings of other people, connecting deeply with them and taking time to imagine what it feels like to live in their shoes (John 1:1–14; 2 Corinthians 8:9; Philippians 2:3–5).   1 2 3 4

2. People close to me would describe me as a responsive listener (Proverbs 10:19; 29:11; James 1:19).   1 2 3 4

3. When I confront someone who has hurt or wronged me, I speak more in the first person ("I" and "me") about how I am feeling rather than speak in blaming tones ("you" or "they") about what was done (Proverbs 25:11; Ephesians 4:29–32).   1 2 3 4

4. I have little interest in making snap judgments about other people (Matthew 7:1–5).   1 2 3 4

5. People would describe me as someone who makes "loving well" my number one aim (John 13:34–35; 1 Corinthians 13).   1 2 3 4

Mark 5 Total _____

Mark 6. Break the Power of the Past

1. I resolve conflict in a clear, direct, and respectful way, avoiding unhealthy behaviors I may have learned growing up in my family, such as painful putdowns, avoidance, escalating tensions, or going to a third party rather than to the person directly (Matthew 18:15–18).   1 2 3 4

2. I am intentional at working through the impact of significant "earthquake" events from the past that have shaped my present, such as the death of a family member, an unexpected pregnancy, divorce, addiction, or financial disaster (Genesis 50:20; Psalm 51).   1 2 3 4

3. I am able to thank God for all my past experiences, seeing how he has used them to uniquely shape me into who I am (Genesis 50:20; Romans 8:28–30).   1 2 3 4

4. I can see how certain "generational sins" have been passed down to me through my family history, including character flaws, lies, secrets, ways of coping with pain, and unhealthy tendencies in relating to others (Exodus 20:5; cf. Genesis 20:2; 26:7; 27:19; 37:1–33).   1 2 3 4

5. I don't need approval from others to feel good about myself (Proverbs 29:25; Galatians 1:10).   1 2 3 4

6. I take responsibility and ownership for my past rather than blame others (John 5:5–7).   1 2 3 4

Mark 6 Total _____

	Not very true	Sometimes true	Mostly true	Very true

Mark 7. Lead out of Weakness and Vulnerability

1. I often admit when I'm wrong, readily asking forgiveness from others (Matthew 5:23–24).   1 2 3 4

2. I am able to speak freely about my weaknesses, failures, and mistakes (2 Corinthians 12:7–12).   1 2 3 4

3. Others would readily describe me as approachable, gentle, open, and transparent (Galatians 5:22–23; 1 Corinthians 13:1–6).   1 2 3 4

4. Those close to me would say that I am not easily offended or hurt (Matthew 5:39–42; 1 Corinthians 13:5).   1 2 3 4

5. I am consistently open to hearing and applying constructive criticism and feedback that others might have for me (Proverbs 10:17; 17:10; 25:12).   1 2 3 4

6. I am rarely judgmental or critical of others (Matthew 7:1–5).   1 2 3 4

7. Others would say that I am slow to speak, quick to listen, and good at seeing things from their perspective (James 1:19–20).   1 2 3 4

Mark 7 Total _____

Tally Your Assessment Results

For each group of questions:

- Add your responses to get the total for that group.

- Transfer your totals to the the right column of the chart on page 22.

- Plot your answers and connect the dots to create a graph on the bottom portion of page 22, following the sample at the top of the same page.

- Read the descriptions on pages 22–23 to learn more about your level of emotional health in each area. What patterns do you discern?

SAMPLE

Marks of Emotionally Healthy Discipleship   Totals

Mark 1. Be Before You Do   20/24

Mark 2. Follow the Crucified, Not the Americanized, Jesus   9/20

Mark 3. Receive God's Gift of Limits   10/24

Mark 4. Discover the Treasures Buried in Grief and Loss   13/20

Mark 5. Make Love the Measure of Spiritual Maturity   16/20

Mark 6. Break the Power of the Past   14/24

Mark 7. Lead out of Weakness and Vulnerability   21/28

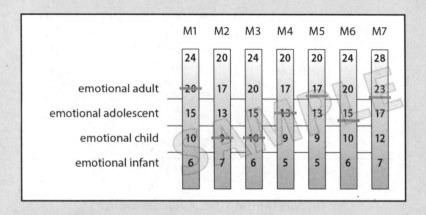

	M1	M2	M3	M4	M5	M6	M7
	24	20	24	20	20	24	28
emotional adult	20	17	20	17	17	20	23
emotional adolescent	15	13	15	13	13	15	17
emotional child	10	9	10	9	9	10	12
emotional infant	6	7	6	5	5	6	7

Marks of Emotionally Healthy Discipleship   Totals

Mark 1. Be Before You Do   __/24
Mark 2. Follow the Crucified, Not the Americanized, Jesus   __/20
Mark 3. Receive God's Gift of Limits   __/24
Mark 4. Discover the Treasures Buried in Grief and Loss   __/20
Mark 5. Make Love the Measure of Spiritual Maturity   __/20
Mark 6. Break the Power of the Past   __/24
Mark 7. Lead out of Weakness and Vulnerability   __/28

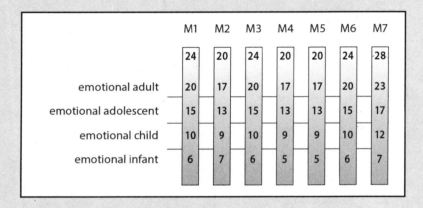

	M1	M2	M3	M4	M5	M6	M7
	24	20	24	20	20	24	28
emotional adult	20	17	20	17	17	20	23
emotional adolescent	15	13	15	13	13	15	17
emotional child	10	9	10	9	9	10	12
emotional infant	6	7	6	5	5	6	7

Understanding Your Assessment:
Levels of Emotional Maturity

Being an emotionally healthy disciple is not an all-or-nothing condition; it operates on a continuum that ranges from mild to severe, and may change from one season of life and ministry to the next. As you read through the descriptions below, what stands out to you? Wherever you find yourself, the good news is that you can make progress and become an increasingly more mature disciple. So even if your current state of discipleship is sobering, don't be discouraged. If someone like me can learn and grow through all the failures and mistakes I've made, it is possible for anyone to make progress.

Here are some observations to help you better understand your assessment results.

Emotional infant. I look for other people to take care of me emotionally and spiritually. I often have difficulty in describing and experiencing my feelings in healthy ways and rarely enter the emotional world of others. I am consistently driven by a need for instant gratification, often using others as objects to meet my needs. People sometimes perceive me as inconsiderate and insensitive. I am uncomfortable with silence or being alone. When trials, hardships, or difficulties come, I want to quit God and the Christian life. I sometimes experience God at church and when I am with other Christians, but rarely when I am at work or home.

Emotional child. When life is going my way, I am content. However, as soon as disappointment or stress enter the picture, I quickly unravel inside. I often take things personally, interpreting disagreements or criticism as a personal offense. When I don't get my way, I often complain, withdraw, manipulate, drag my feet, become sarcastic, or take revenge. I often end up living off the spirituality of other people because I am so overloaded and distracted. My prayer life is primarily talking to God, telling him what to do and how to fix my problems. Prayer is more a duty than a delight.

Emotional adolescent. I don't like it when others question me. I often make quick judgments and interpretations of people's behavior. I withhold forgiveness from those who sin against me, avoiding or cutting them off when they do something to hurt me. I subconsciously keep records on the love I give out. I have trouble really listening to another person's pain, disappointments, or needs without becoming preoccupied with myself. I sometimes find myself too busy to spend adequate time nourishing my spiritual life. I attend church and serve others but enjoy few delights in Christ. My Christian life is still primarily about doing, not being with him. Prayer continues to be mostly me talking with little silence, solitude, or listening to God.

Emotional adult. I respect and love others without having to change them or becoming judgmental. I value people for who they are, not for what they can give me or how they behave. I take responsibility for my own thoughts, feelings, goals, and actions. I can state my own beliefs and values to those who disagree with me—without becoming adversarial. I am able to accurately self-assess my limits, strengths, and weaknesses. I am deeply convinced that I am absolutely loved by Christ and do not look to others to tell me I'm okay. I am able to integrate *doing* for God and *being* with him (Mary and Martha). My Christian life has moved beyond simply serving Christ to loving him and enjoying communion with him.

GROUP MEETING

Daily Office (10 minutes)

Do one of the Daily Offices from Week 1 of *Emotionally Healthy Relationships Day by Day* to begin your session. (**Leaders, please see point number two in the "General Guidelines" on page 160.**)

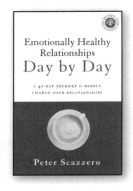

Introduction (2 minutes)

The essence of true Christian spirituality is to love well. This requires that we experience connection with God, with ourselves, and with other people. God invites us to practice his presence in our daily lives. At the same time, he invites us to "practice the presence of people," within an awareness of his presence, in our daily relationships. Sadly, the two are rarely brought together.[2]

The Christians in the church in Corinth failed to make that connection. They were zealous, diligent, and absolutely committed to having God as Lord of their lives. They had the faith to move mountains, gave great amounts of money to the poor, and were incredibly gifted, but they did not love people. They did not link loving God to loving people.

Jesus always integrated the presence of God with the practice of loving people. He summarized the entire Bible for us in light of this unbreakable union: "'Love the Lord your God with all your heart and with all your soul and with all your mind.' This is the first and greatest commandment. And the second is like it: 'Love your neighbor as yourself.' All the Law and the Prophets hang on these two commandments" (Matthew 22:37–40).

Growing Connected (10 minutes)

1. Take a minute each to share your name, what you hope to get out of this course, and what makes you feel fully alive.

Bible Study (10 minutes)

The Corinthian church was a gifted, influential, intelligent (high IQ—intellectual intelligence) church that was weak in its ability to love well (low EQ—emotional intelligence). Read aloud 1 Corinthians 13:1–3 (NRSV):

> If I speak in the tongues of mortals and of angels, but do not have love, I am a noisy gong or a clanging cymbal. 2 And if I have prophetic powers, and understand all mysteries and all knowledge, and if I have all faith, so as to remove mountains, but do not have love, I am nothing. 3 If I give away all my possessions, and if I hand over my body so that I may boast, but do not have love, I gain nothing.

2. How do you understand the words, "If I have the gift of prophecy and can fathom all mysteries and all knowledge, and if I have a faith that can move mountains, but have not love, *I am nothing*" (emphasis added)?

3. How might this passage clash with your understanding of spiritual maturity?

4. As you think back over the past week, can you give one or two examples of how you separated your love for God from your love for people?

▶ VIDEO: Take Your Community Temperature Reading (20 minutes)

Video Notes

Something Was Wrong; Something Was Missing

- People were growing in their love for God, but it wasn't translating into their love for other people.
- The quality of love inside the church was not really that different from the quality of love outside the church.
- We hit this wall.
- What is missing in our spiritual formation/discipleship and the way we handle our relationships?

We Call This Emotionally Healthy Spirituality

- Emotional health and spiritual maturity are inseparable. It is not possible to be spiritually mature while remaining emotionally immature.

  > "Love the Lord your God with all your heart and with all your soul and with all your mind." . . . And the second is like it: "Love your neighbor as yourself." (Matthew 22:37–39)

- Loving God and loving others is the essence of true spirituality.

  > If I speak in the tongues of men or of angels, but do have not love . . . and if I have a faith that can move mountains, but do have not love, I am nothing. (1 Corinthians 13:1–2)

- Paul links true spirituality with our ability to love other people well.
- We need to give people the skills to "do" the Bible.
- Every Christian needs practical skills in order to grow into emotional/spiritual adulthood.
- To get these skills you must experience or practice them.

Eight Emotionally Healthy Skills

1. The Community Temperature Reading (CTR)
2. Stop Mind Reading and Clarify Expectations
3. Genogram Your Family
4. Explore the Iceberg
5. Listen Incarnationally (or Incarnational Listening)
6. Climb the Ladder of Integrity
7. Fight Cleanly (or Clean Fighting)
8. Develop a "Rule of Life" to Implement Emotionally Healthy Skills

RELATIONSHIPS IN THE NEW FAMILY OF JESUS

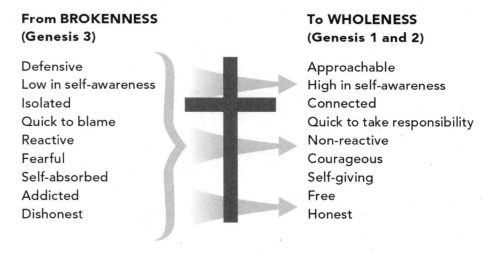

From BROKENNESS
(Genesis 3)

Defensive
Low in self-awareness
Isolated
Quick to blame
Reactive
Fearful
Self-absorbed
Addicted
Dishonest

To WHOLENESS
(Genesis 1 and 2)

Approachable
High in self-awareness
Connected
Quick to take responsibility
Non-reactive
Courageous
Self-giving
Free
Honest

Community Temperature Reading (CTR): What Is It?

- This is the building block for the rest of the skills that follow.
- **The purpose:** To discover and express your God-given voice and to build healthy relationships with others.
- It's about brief sharing.

The Five Categories

1. Appreciations
   - We think them in our heads but often only say them when someone has gone above and beyond the call of duty.
   - Some families and cultures never express appreciations.
   - Appreciations are important to the life of any community or relationship.

     > e.g., "I appreciate you waiting for me last night when I was running late."

     > e.g., "I appreciate you arriving early and getting the coffee ready before the meeting."

2. Puzzles
   - We use them when we don't want to make negative assumptions about people, especially when we don't have all the information.
   - Puzzles prevent us from jumping to conclusions and negatively interpreting what is going on around us.
   - Puzzles give us an opportunity to slow down and ask questions instead of making judgments.
   - *Puzzle* is a loving word.

     > e.g., Instead of being upset and not saying anything at all or angrily saying, "Why didn't you return my phone call?" you can say, "I'm *puzzled* as to why you didn't return my phone call."

     > e.g., Instead of thinking, *No one washed the dishes last night. I live with a bunch of slobs!* you can say, "I'm *puzzled* as to why you left your dirty dishes in the sink last night."

3. Complaints with Possible Solutions
   - All relationships have complaints or things they don't like. This is normal.
   - Two challenges with complaints: (1) Some of our families grew up with an unwritten rule: If you don't have anything nice to say, don't say anything at all. (2) It is very easy to complain and not take *any* responsibility for a possible solution.
   - The purpose of "Complaints with Possible Solutions" is to help you with small irritations and annoyances that arise each day.
   - Use the phrase "I notice . . . and I prefer . . ."[3]

     e.g., "*I notice* you often leave the lights on in our apartment when you leave, and *I prefer* you turn them off."

     e.g., "*I notice* our meetings start late, and *I prefer* we start at the agreed upon time."

   - The person with the complaint takes responsibility for a possible solution.
   - Keep complaints light in the Community Temperature Reading.

4. New Information
   - This can take many forms—events, appointments, new decisions, achievements, opportunities, or activities. Relationships can only grow when people know what is happening in each other's lives, both the trivial as well as the important.

     e.g., "Our professor moved the exam so I can go to the movies this week."

     e.g., "I'm exploring a different job within my company!"

5. Hopes and Wishes
   - Hopes and wishes offer windows into our unique souls, revealing significant parts of who we are.
   - Family life in particular becomes richer as we support and listen to each other's hopes and dreams.

     e.g., "I hope we can get away for vacation this year."

     e.g., "I hope to get a master's degree in nursing someday."

Pete and Geri Model a CTR

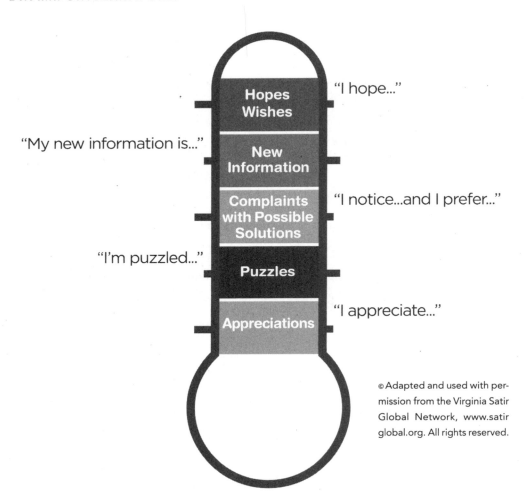

"I hope..."

"My new information is..."

"I notice...and I prefer..."

"I'm puzzled..."

"I appreciate..."

Ⅱ *Pause the Video*

Workbook Activities (25 minutes)

Partner Activity: CTR (10 minutes)

1. Pair up with one other person—or with two others if there is an uneven number in your group. In order to make the practice of this skill real, role-play with your partner if needed, letting them know who they are filling in for (e.g., a friend, boss, coworker, sibling) in each of the categories.

2. Review the Guidelines for the CTR:
   - Face each other as you share.
   - Take turns sharing back and forth.
   - Keep sharing light and brief.
   - Use only the sentence stems given.
   - Do not interrupt or respond. Only respond to puzzles or complaints with a few words if appropriate.

3. Using the graphic of the Community Temperature Reading on page 30, begin at the bottom of the thermometer, with "Appreciations," and take turns.

4. Work on only one category at a time. Feel free to skip a category if nothing comes to your mind.

5. Keep it light, especially with the "Complaints and Possible Solutions."

Small Group Sharing (10 minutes)

In groups of three or four:

1. How did your family of origin share appreciations? Complaints? Hopes and wishes?

2. What was it like for you to express yourself in these different categories?

3. Which was easiest for you? Which was most difficult for you?

▶ VIDEO: Closing Summary (6 minutes)

Video Notes

Healthy ways of relating clash with most families and cultures. This is one practical way to put off the old self and put on the new self in Christ (Ephesians 4:22–24).

The CTR is a flexible, elastic tool that can be used one-on-one or in a group setting.

It can be used with children/families, with friends, at the workplace, in classrooms, or in a small group.

How it is used is dependent on two factors:
1. Time: How much time do you have? Feel free to use only one or two elements if time is limited.
2. Environment: If there is a lot of tension in the group, you may want to skip "Complaints and Possible Solutions."

Remember, the CTR is meant to be used as a tool, not a weapon.

Practice the Community Temperature Reading two to three times a week throughout the course.

Conclusion: When we try to love in our own strength, we discover we can't. We naturally fall back to unhealthy ways of relating, especially under stress. We need Jesus' love to flow *into* us if it is to flow *out* of us.

That is why developing and deepening your relationship with Jesus by using *EH Relationships Day by Day* is core to this course.

Optional Session Wrap-up (5 minutes)

Together with your small group, ask any questions of clarification regarding this session and then briefly close in prayer.

PERSONAL ACTION STEP

Decide when you will practice this skill before the next session. (We recommend two to three times.) Write your response below.

I plan on practicing the CTR:

With whom? _____

When? _____

Between-Sessions Personal Study

Session One

Read the pre-session assignment for Session 2 on pages 40–42. Use the space provided to note any insights or questions you might want to bring to the next group session.

Prayerfully read Week 1 of the *Emotionally Healthy Relationships Day by Day* devotional, "Take Your Community Temperature Reading." Use the space provided to answer the Questions to Consider and/or to journal your thoughts each day.

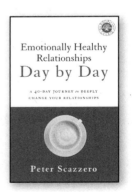

DAY 1   Questions to Consider:

When can you set aside uninterrupted time each day to begin cultivating an awareness of the presence of God?

Whose beauty might you be bypassing because you are too busy or distracted?

DAY 2 Questions to Consider:

In what areas of life might your pursuit of "getting things done" or "doing right things" be more important to you than seeking a loving relationship with God and others?

Consider your present balance between solitude and community. To what degree is it adequate for you to be growing in love for God, others, and yourself?

DAY 3 Questions to Consider:

What difference might it make in your day to remember that, in every moment you turn your heart to God—including this very moment—he is waiting for you and loving you first?

Think back over the last few days. In what way(s) did your to-do list, distractibility, or perfectionism keep you from loving and enjoying Jesus or the people around you?

DAY 4 Questions to Consider:

In what subtle or perhaps even unconscious ways might you be judging or despising someone in your life?

In your own life, how might it be true that falling in love with Jesus and staying in love with Jesus will decide everything? How could it change you, as well as your relationships?

DAY 5 Questions to Consider:

What two or three things from the past week are you most thankful for? (For example, good health or healing, people in your life, possessions, opportunities, trials, closed doors, spiritual blessings, etc.) Express your heartfelt gratitude to God for these gifts.

What is your biggest challenge in integrating these two loves in this season of your life?

Stop Mind Reading and Clarify Expectations

Session Two

PRE-SESSION READING

God has given us an inner guidance system to move through life—thinking and feeling. It is essential that we pay attention to our thoughts and feelings. But then we must think about what to do with them. Knowing when to follow our feelings and when *not* to is indispensable if we are to grow up into spiritual adulthood in Christ.

God is omniscient—he knows all things about all situations. And God alone knows what is going on in the minds of other people. Yet, we routinely play God when we make assumptions about another person or interpret a certain behavior without verifying the facts. These assumptions unleash much needless pain and confusion. In fact, the application of these two simple skills hold within them the key to preventing large-scale faulty thinking in your family, workplace, and church.

Imagine your husband, who usually calls you while at work, doesn't call one day. You begin to wonder if he is angry with you. You did have an argument last night, but you thought it got resolved. You assume the worst. All day long you stew over his apparent immature behavior. How dare he give you the cold shoulder!

You choose to ignore him when he arrives home and go to bed without saying good night. He remains at the kitchen table doing paperwork, not asking if anything is wrong. This confirms your hypothesis about his immaturity. Things are even worse than you thought.

"Who knows what tomorrow will bring?" you mutter to yourself in resignation as you turn off the light. The truth, you learn later, is that he did not call because of an emergency at work. Yet you created an intricate scenario in your mind that was not true.

Imagine you are part of a church ministry team planning a big event. As director, you are exchanging quite a few emails with the rest of the team. You notice that one of the team members, Ken, who used to be warm and friendly, now shoots back terse replies. You interpret this as passive-aggressive behavior and assume he must be upset with you for something. Two can play at that game, so you fire off a few short, curt emails in return.

Soon thereafter, you speak to Ken on the phone. He is warm and engaging. You realize you wrongly "read his mind" in interpreting his emails negatively. You caused yourself unnecessary angst and murdered him in your heart.

In both scenarios, you spiral downward by negatively interpreting the behavior of another and making assumptions about what they're thinking. These turn into hidden landmines in relationships. Slowly, you build up resentments. You hurt yourself. You build invisible walls to keep others out. And worst of all, you quench God's Spirit within you.

Think of a person with whom you might be mind reading or about whom you are making assumptions you have not verified. At an appropriate time, ask them the following question: "May I have permission to read your mind?" or, "Can I check out an assumption I have?" or, "Do I have permission to check out my thinking with you?"

Once they say yes, consider the examples below for ways to check out your thinking and stop the mind reading . . .

- "I think that you think I'm responsible for the Christmas shopping this year. Is that correct?"
- "I'm wondering if you think that I think you are a bad person for not remembering my birthday. Is that correct?"
- "I noticed that you didn't return my phone calls for a few days. That's unusual for you, so I'm wondering if there is something wrong."
- "I'm puzzled that you gave Jane and Richard big hugs but passed me over. I'm wondering if I said or did something to upset you."
- "I noticed you didn't call me from work today. Is everything all right, or is there still some lingering tension after our disagreement last night?"

The stories we tell ourselves have an enormous impact on our feelings. Consider the difference of what goes on in your mind when a friend, who agrees to meet you for dinner, is forty minutes late. How different are your feelings when you tell yourself, "Maybe he had an accident driving here," or "This relationship is clearly more important to me than it is to him!" Each interpretation generates a different feeling. Why? Because our feelings are closely related to the story we tell ourselves about the things going on around us.

To quit faulty thinking and maintain good emotional and spiritual health, we must make an intentional decision to stop mind reading and to verify our assumptions by talking to people—*in person* instead of in our heads.

—*The Emotionally Healthy Woman*, pages 184–187, 189

GROUP MEETING

Daily Office (10 minutes)

Do one of the Daily Offices from Week 2 of *Emotionally Healthy Relationships Day by Day* to begin your session. (**Leaders, please see point number two in "General Guidelines" on page 160.**)

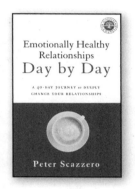

Introduction (2 minutes)

The ninth commandment reads: "You shall not give false testimony against your neighbor" (Exodus 20:16). Every time we make an assumption about someone who has hurt or disappointed us, without confirming it, we believe a lie about this person in our head. Because we have not checked it out with him or her, it is very possible that we are believing something untrue. It is also likely that we will pass that false assumption around to others.

When we leave reality for a mental creation of our own doing (hidden assumptions), we create a counterfeit world. When we do this, it can properly be said that we exclude God from our lives because God does not exist outside of reality and truth. In doing so we wreck relationships by creating endless confusion and conflict. The Bible has much to say about not taking on the role of judge to others (Matthew 7:1–5).

The application of these two simple skills—Stop Mind Reading and Clarify Expectations—holds within it the key to preventing large-scale misunderstandings in your friendships, family, workplace, and church. These skills provide practical help for loving others well by eliminating untold numbers of conflicts in our relationships.

Growing Connected (10 minutes)

1. *Day by Day* Debrief: God says: "Be still and know that I am God" (Psalm 46:10). This requires silence yet the practice of silence may be the weakest link in our discipleship today. What challenges are you experiencing as you begin and end your *EH Relationships Day by Day* readings with silence? (7 minutes)

2. Turn to the person next to you and share a recent unmet expectation you had of someone (e.g., your phone call, text, or email was not returned). What story did you tell yourself?

Bible Study (10 minutes)

The book of Proverbs is filled with practical wisdom about holy restraint and not jumping to conclusions before we have all the facts. Read Proverbs 18:2, 13, 15, and 17.

"Fools find no pleasure in understanding but delight in airing their own opinions." (Proverbs 18:2)

"To answer before listening—that is folly and shame." (Proverbs 18:13)

"The heart of the discerning acquires knowledge; the ears of the wise seek it out." (Proverbs 18:15)

"In a lawsuit the first to speak seems right, until someone comes forward and cross-examines." (Proverbs 18:17)

3. Based on the first three proverbs listed above, what are the differences between a fool and a wise person with a discerning heart?

4. Can you briefly share a specific situation when what you were thinking or feeling about someone was untrue, or you misinterpreted the behavior of another person without checking it out? What did you end up believing incorrectly until you heard the whole story (see Proverbs 18:17)?

▶ VIDEO: Stop Mind Reading and Clarify Expectations (6 minutes)

Each of these skills is meant to help us grow as disciples of Jesus.

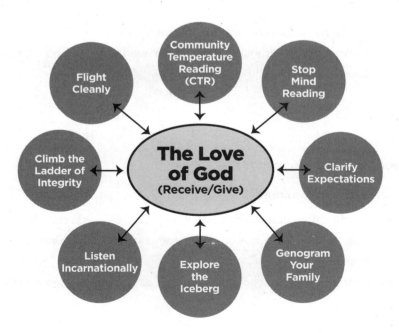

- Stop Mind Reading and Clarify Expectations revolve around eliminating the assumptions and misunderstandings that can cause havoc and destroy relationships.
- These skills are based on the biblical truth of the ninth commandment:

> "You shall not give false testimony [witness] against your neighbor."
> (Exodus 20:16)

Stop Mind Reading

- **The purpose:** To clarify what another person is thinking instead of making assumptions.
- **Key principle:** Never assume you know what a person is thinking or feeling.[1]
- How you can stop mind reading:
  1. Ask permission to read his/her mind.
  2. Say, "I think you think . . . Is that correct?"

Pete and Geri Model "Stop Mind Reading"

Dangers of Mind Reading

- We tell ourselves stories about others that aren't true.
- Making assumptions without checking them out damages friendships, families, and relationships in churches and workplaces.

(II) *Pause the Video*

Workbook Activities (6 minutes)

Individual Activity (2 minutes)

1. Consider the different relationship areas of your life—work, church, family (marriage, children, parents, siblings, extended family), friendships, neighbors, or roommates.
2. Pick one where you might be "mind reading" or making an assumption.

3. Write down the person's name (or initials) and the assumption you have.

Partner Activity (4 minutes)

Turn to one person in the group. Ask him/her to sit in for the person whose name you wrote down, and then practice this skill.

1. First ask:
   - "May I have permission to read your mind?" or
   - "Can I check out an assumption I have?"
2. After the person answers yes, say:
   - "I think that you think . . . Is that correct?" or
   - "I am wondering . . . Is that correct?"

(▶) *Resume the Video* (10 minutes)

Video Notes
Clarify Expectations

- Similar to the Stop Mind Reading skill, Clarify Expectations is about eliminating confusion, pain, and disappointment in relationships.
- **The purpose:** To recognize whether certain expectations are valid or not, and to clarify our expectations with others.
- Expectations come from many sources: families, cultures, TV, the internet, fairy tales, billboards, schools, etc.

The Problem with Many of Our Expectations

1. **Unconscious:** We have expectations of others that we don't even know we have. We often don't know we have the expectation until we are disappointed.
2. **Unrealistic:** We have expectations that are not reasonable.

3. **Unspoken:** We're conscious of them, and they may be realistic, but they are not spoken.
4. **Un-agreed Upon:** We have expectations of others that they did not agree to, or others have expectations of us that we did not agree to.

Confusion around expectations exists in:
- Workplaces
- Homes and families
- Neighborhoods
- Churches

The Million-Dollar Question

- What expectations do we have a right to have and what expectations do we not have a right to have? In other words, what is a valid expectation and what is an invalid expectation?
- Sometimes we don't even know we have an expectation until we become angry or disappointed.
- What makes an expectation valid? Valid expectations are:
  1. **Conscious:** I am aware of my expectation.
  2. **Realistic:** This means there is evidence to support that the expectation is reasonable. Either it has been done in the past or the person has the capacity and willingness to do it.
  3. **Spoken:** I have expressed the expectation clearly.
  4. **Agreed Upon:** The other person has agreed to the expectation by saying "yes."

Key principle: An expectation is only valid when it is mutually agreed upon. The exceptions to this key principle are expectations between a parent and child (e.g., expected chores); employer/employee contracts; and marriage vows of faithfulness.

⏸ *Pause the Video*

Workbook Activity (3 minutes)

Individual Activity (3 minutes)

1. Think of a recent, simple expectation you had that went unmet and made you angry, disappointed, or confused. (For example: Someone didn't return your phone call; a close friend didn't send you a birthday card; your extended family holiday gathering was filled with tension; your roommate did not take out the garbage; or, as the last one home, your son did not turn off the lights.) Write it below.

2. Use the following checklist to clarify the expectation in your own mind:
    *   **Conscious:** Were you aware you had this expectation?
    *   **Realistic:** Is this expectation reasonable? Why? Or why not? What is the specific evidence that this person (or these people) can, or will, do this? For example: If your holiday with your family each year is always filled with tension, what has changed so that this year might be different? If your close friends do not normally send you a birthday card, what has changed this year so that you can realistically expect a different outcome?
    *   **Spoken:** Have you clearly spoken the expectation, or do you just think the other person should know?
    *   **Agreed Upon:** Has the other person agreed to the expectation?

REMEMBER THIS PRINCIPLE: Expectations are only valid when they have been mutually agreed upon.

As you watch the following video segment, you will see examples of expectations that are not clarified ("The Wrong Way"). In the final example, you will see what it looks like to clarify an expectation well ("The Right Way"). Note the differences as you watch.

▶ *Resume the Video* (2 minutes)

Clarify Expectations: The Wrong Way

Clarify Expectations: The Right Way

⏸ *Pause the Video*

Workbook Activities (25 Minutes)

Partner Activity (15 minutes)

1. Find a partner. Share the expectation you wrote down in the earlier Individual Activity and whom it applies to. Your partner will role-play as that person. If you have a "live" situation with someone in the group, partner with him/her.

2. Practice clarifying your expectation and see if it is agreed upon. Here are some possible sentence stems to help you begin:
   - I'd like to clarify an expectation I have of you . . . Is this correct?
   - I expect . . . because . . . Can we agree to that?
   - I wonder . . . Are you willing?
   - I'd like to check out an assumption I've made . . . Is this true?

3. Take a few minutes and then switch roles.

4. Repeat the skill a second time using a different scenario.

Small Group Sharing (10 minutes)

In groups of three or four:

1. What was this experience like for you?

2. Where else in your life might you have expectations, or be making assumptions of others, that you need to clarify—in your workplace, school, family, or friendships?

   What is an expectation someone might have of you that needs clarification? What might your next steps be?

▶ VIDEO: Closing Summary (3 minutes)

Video Notes

Many issues are resolved by simply clarifying expectations around them. Others require negotiation. This will be covered in Session 7 with the Fight Cleanly (or Clean Fighting) skill.

Three Common Questions

1. What do I do when someone cannot meet my expectation?
2. What do I do if I have an agreed upon expectation with someone and they don't do it?
3. What do I do if God doesn't meet my expectations?

Optional Session Wrap-up (5 minutes)

Together with your small group, ask any questions of clarification regarding this session and then briefly close in prayer.

PERSONAL ACTION STEP

Decide when you will practice this skill before the next session. (We recommend two to three times.) Write your response below.

I plan on practicing the Stop Mind Reading and Clarify Expectations skills:

With whom? _____

When? _____

Between-Sessions Personal Study

Session Two

Read the pre-session assignment for Session 3 on pages 58–60. Use the space provided to note any insights or questions you might want to bring to the next group session.

Prayerfully read Week 2 of the *Emotionally Healthy Relationships Day by Day* devotional, "Stop Mind Reading and Clarify Expectations." Use the space provided to answer the Questions to Consider and/or to journal your thoughts each day.

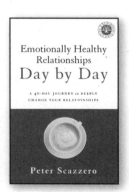

DAY 1 Questions to Consider:

How might you follow a "little way" of love today in a situation where you might otherwise express annoyance, impatience, or frustration?

In what kind of situations is it most difficult for you to pause and give thought to your ways?

DAY 2 Questions to Consider:

Today, how might you accept the Father's invitation to be silent, "to go off to a solitary place" as Jesus did?

Think back over the past few days. In what subtle or not-so-subtle ways did you bend the truth to make yourself look better or avoid someone's disapproval? How was your integrity compromised as a result?

DAY 3 Questions to Consider:

What first comes to mind in response to these words from God for you today: "In repentance and rest is your salvation, in quietness and trust is your strength"?

To which of the three forms of faulty thinking ("It's all or nothing," "I'm offended," "Things will never change") are you most susceptible? How has it resulted in unnecessary pain or broken relationships in your life?

DAY 4 Questions to Consider:

What seeds from God might be coming to rest in your mind and heart today, particularly through a relationship difficulty which you are experiencing?

In what relationship are you making an assumption that may not be true? What small step can you take today to clarify the truth with that person?

DAY 5 Questions to Consider:

Identify one situation in your life in which God appears to be saying no or is failing to meet your expectations. How does your response compare to David's?

Who are you tempted to blame for an unhappy or difficult situation in your life? How might you use your God-given freedom to take greater responsibility for one of your choices today?

Genogram Your Family

Session Three

PRE-SESSION READING

When the Bible uses the word *family*, it refers to our entire extended family over three to four generations. That means your family, in the biblical sense, includes all your brothers, sisters, uncles, aunts, grandparents, great-grandparents, great-uncles and aunts, and significant others going back to the mid-1800s!

While we are affected by powerful external events and circumstances through our earthly lives, our families are the most powerful group to which we will ever belong. Even those who left home as young adults, determined to "break" from their family histories, soon find that their family's way of "doing" life follows them wherever they go.

What happens in one generation often repeats itself in the next. The consequences of actions and decisions taken in one generation affect those who follow.

For this reason it is common to observe certain patterns from one generation to the next such as divorce, alcoholism, addictive behavior, sexual abuse, poor marriages, one child running off, mistrust of authority, pregnancy out of wedlock, an inability to sustain stable relationships, etc. Scientists and sociologists have been debating for decades whether this is a result of "nature" (i.e., our DNA) or "nurture" (i.e., our environment) or both. The Bible doesn't answer this question. It only states that this is a "mysterious law of God's universe."[1]

Consider the following:

God, in the giving of the Ten Commandments, connected this reality to the very nature of who he is: "You shall not make for yourself an idol . . . for I, the LORD your God, am a jealous God, *punishing the children for the sin of the fathers to the third and fourth generation of those who hate me, but showing love to a thousand generations of those who love me and keep my commandments*" (Exodus 20:4–6, emphasis added).

God repeated the same truth again when Moses asked to see God's glory: "And he passed in front of Moses, proclaiming, 'The LORD, the LORD, the compassionate and gracious God, slow to anger, abounding in love and faithfulness. . . . *Yet he does not leave the guilty unpunished; he punishes the children and their children for the sin of the fathers to the third and fourth generation'"* (Exodus 34:6–7, emphasis added).

When David murdered Uriah in order to marry his wife Bathsheba, God declared, *"Now, therefore, the sword will never depart from your house, because you despised me and took the wife of Uriah the Hittite to be your own"* (2 Samuel 12:10, emphasis added). Family tensions, sibling rivalry, and internal strife marked his children, grandchildren, and great-grandchildren for generations.

Family patterns from the past are played out in our present relationships without us necessarily being aware of it. Someone may look like an individual acting alone—but they are really players in a larger family system that may go back, as the Bible says, three to four generations. Unfortunately, it is not possible to erase the negative effects of our history. This family history lives inside all of us, especially in those who attempt to bury it. The price we pay for this flight is high. Only the truth sets us free. . . .

The great news of Christianity is that your family of origin does not determine your future. God does! What has gone before you is not your destiny! The most significant language in the New Testament for becoming a Christian is "adoption into the family of God." It is a radical new beginning. When we place our faith in Christ, we are spiritually reborn by the Holy Spirit into the family of Jesus. We are transferred out of darkness into the kingdom of light.

The apostle Paul used the image of Roman adoption to communicate this profound truth, emphasizing we are now in a new and permanent relationship with a new Father. God becomes our Father. Our debts (sins) are cancelled. We are given a new name (Christian), a new inheritance (freedom, hope, glory, the resources of heaven), and new brothers and sisters (other Christians) (Ephesians 1).

Jesus' mother and brothers arrived at a house where he was teaching, looking for him to come outside. Jesus replied to the crowd inside the house sitting at his feet: "'Who are my mother and my brothers?' . . . Then he looked at those seated in a circle around him and said, 'Here are my mother and my brothers! Whoever does God's will is my brother and sister and mother'" (Mark 3:33–35). The church for the believer was now the "first family."[2]

In the ancient world of Jesus, it was extremely important to honor one's mother and father. Jesus demonstrated that, even while hanging on the cross. He entrusted the care of his mother to the apostle John. Yet Jesus was direct and clear in calling people to a first loyalty to himself over their biological families, saying, "Anyone who loves his father or mother more than me is not worthy of me" (Matthew 10:37). Discipleship, then, is the putting off of the sinful patterns and habits of our families of origin and being transformed to live as members of Christ's family.

This is the Christian life. God's intention is that we grow up into mature men and women transformed by the indwelling presence of Christ. We honor our parents, culture, and histories but obey God.

Every disciple, then, has to look at the brokenness and sin of his or her family and culture. The problem is that few of us have reflected honestly on the impact of our family of origin and other major "earthquake" events in our histories.

Philosopher George Santanya said it well: "Those who cannot learn from the past are doomed to repeat it." For example, perhaps your family defined success by profession or education or money. Maybe there were underlying messages that in order to be loved, cared for, or accepted you needed to do certain behaviors. This impacted your view of yourself (i.e., your self-esteem).

In God's family, success is defined as being faithful to God's purpose and plan for your life. We are called to seek first his kingdom and righteousness (Matthew 6:33). Everything else, he promises, will be added to us. Moreover, God declares we are loveable. We are good enough in Christ (Luke 15:21–24).

Discipleship, then, is working these truths into our practical, everyday lives.

Sadly, when we look deep beneath the surface of our lives, most of us are not doing anything fundamentally different from what our families did. God's intention, however, is that our local churches and parishes are to be places where, slowly but surely, we are re-parented in doing life Christ's way.

God intends that his new community of people be the place where we are set free. This requires recognizing the sad reality that all of us bring to our new community our old "Egyptian" ways of living and relating.

—*Emotionally Healthy Spirituality*, Updated Edition, pages 73–75, 82–84

GROUP MEETING

Daily Office (10 minutes)

Do one of the Daily Offices from Week 3 of *Emotionally Healthy Relationships Day by Day* to begin your session. **(Leaders, please see point number two in "General Guidelines" on page 160.)**

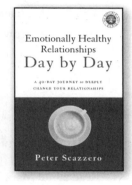

Introduction (2 minutes)

The New Testament describes becoming a Christian as a spiritual rebirth through which we are adopted into a new family—the family of Jesus. God does forgive the past, but he does *not* erase it. We are given a new start, but we still come in as babies drinking milk and are expected to grow up and become mature adults who love well.

We all come into the family of Jesus with brokenness and wounds from being born into a broken world and imperfect families. God's intention is to heal us, but we must first become aware of what needs to be changed in us.

Discipleship, then, must include honest reflection on the positive and negative impacts of our family of origin as well as other major influences in our lives.

This is hard work. But the extent to which we can go back and understand how our history has shaped us will determine, to a large degree, our ability to break destructive patterns and grow in love toward God and people.[3]

Growing Connected (10 minutes)

1. *Day by Day* Debrief: At the heart of this Course is nurturing your relationship with God, especially in silence and Scripture. How was your experience in practicing silence this week?

2. Turn to the person next to you and share what was considered "success" in your family growing up. How did that impact you?

Bible Study (10 minutes)

1. Read aloud Mark 3:31–35 (below). Imagine the scene as Jesus' mother and brothers arrive at the house. Try to picture yourself as part of the story. Where do you find yourself? What are you feeling?

> Then Jesus' mother and brothers arrived. Standing outside, they sent someone in to call him. A crowd was sitting around him, and they told him, "Your mother and brothers are outside looking for you."
>
> "Who are my mother and my brothers?" he asked. Then he looked at those seated in a circle around him and said, "Here are my mother and my brothers! Whoever does God's will is my brother and sister and mother."

2. Describe the qualities of those circled around Jesus inside the house.

3. In vv. 34-35 Jesus emphasizes a loyalty to himself that is greater than our loyalty to our biological family. What might that look like in our everyday life of following him? (e.g. way we deal with money, conflict, relationships)

▶ VIDEO: Genogram Your Family (15 minutes)

Video Notes

A genogram is a visual tool to help us look at the history and dynamics of our family over three to four generations.

The purpose: To become aware of and to break the sinful patterns in your family of origin in order to live out your God-given purpose in the world.

Two Biblical Truths about Families

1. The blessings and sins of our families have an impact lasting for at least three to four generations.

    "He punishes the children...for the sin of the fathers to the third and fourth generation." (Exodus 34:7)

    - The Hebrew word for *punish* means "tends to be repeated." What happens in one generation often repeats itself in the next.

2. Becoming a Christian is to be birthed into a new family and a new culture
    - When we come to Christ, we are birthed and adopted into God's family.

- Discipleship is learning to do life in Jesus' family.
- This is hard work. Why? Jesus may be in your heart, but Grandpa lives in your bones.

Example of Pete and Example of Geri

(❚❚) *Pause the Video*

Workbook Activities (20 minutes)

Individual Activity (15 minutes)

We look at our families not to find fault but to get a realistic picture of what was healthy and unhealthy so we can grow, heal, and mature into our authentic selves in Christ. Use the diagram on the next page to begin constructing your genogram. Because of session time restraints, you may not be able to finish it now.

We are not focusing on our positive legacies in this exercise due to the limits of time as well as our tendency to avoid looking at the negative aspects of our families.

Complete instructions 1–3 below through the eyes of your childhood, from eight to twelve years old. Then use the space provided to respond to the question in number 4.

1. Using the symbols in the following chart, return to your genogram and describe possible relational dynamics between family members.

RELATIONSHIP	RELATIONAL DYNAMICS	SYMBOL
Conflicted	A consistent pattern where issues do not get resolved between people.	□〰〰〰○
Cut Offs	People in the family stop talking to one another or avoid contact.	□—‖—○
Distant/Poor	Low or minimal emotional connection between family members.	□------○
Enmeshment	Pressure is created for family members to think, feel and act alike. There is low tolerance for people to be seperate, to disagree, or be different.	□══════○
Abuse	A severe crossing of personal boundaries - whether it be sexual, emotional, or physical, severely injuring the dignity and humanity of another.	□⨝⨝⨝⨝○

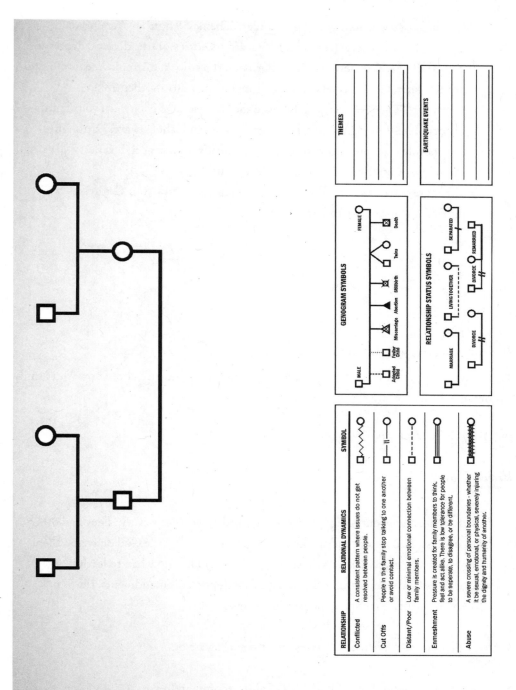

2. On the bottom of your genogram (under "Themes"), note any generational themes that you notice (e.g., addictions, affairs, losses, abuse, divorce, depression, mental illness, abortions, children born out of wedlock, unemployment, physical health issues, family secrets, moving from one place to another, etc.).

3. Below the "Themes" section, also note the "Earthquake Events" in your family history. These are significant, large events that send "shock waves" through your family (e.g., premature death, abuse, suicide, war, cancer, business collapse, infidelity, or immigration from another country).

4. What are one or two insights you learned regarding how your family has impacted who you are today?

Partner Activity (5 minutes)

Turn to one person and share, from question 4, an insight you learned about how your family has impacted who you are today.

▶ *Resume the Video* (5 Minutes)

Video Notes

The Israelites came out of Egypt after four hundred years of slavery. They had other gods, lied, stole, coveted, and worked seven days a week. While God delivered them out of Egypt by grace, Egypt was still deep in them. They now had to learn how to do life as God's new family. So God gave them new commandments, the Ten Commandments, to reshape them as his people.

Key principle: We can only change what we are aware of.

Look at the sample chart of Unbiblical Family Commandments on page 67.

EXAMPLES OF UNBIBLICAL FAMILY COMMANDMENTS

1. MONEY
- MONEY IS THE BEST SOURCE OF SECURITY.
- THE MORE MONEY YOU HAVE, THE MORE IMPORTANT YOU ARE.
- MAKE LOTS OF MONEY TO PROVE YOU "MADE" IT.

2. CONFLICT
- AVOID CONFLICT AT ALL COSTS.
- DON'T GET PEOPLE MAD AT YOU.
- LOUD, ANGRY, CONSTANT FIGHTING IS NORMAL.

3. SEX
- SEX IS NOT TO BE SPOKEN ABOUT OPENLY.
- MEN CAN BE PROMISCUOUS; WOMEN MUST BE CHASTE.

4. GRIEF AND LOSS
- SADNESS IS A SIGN OF WEAKNESS.
- YOU ARE NOT ALLOWED TO BE DEPRESSED.
- GET OVER LOSSES QUICKLY AND MOVE ON.

5. EXPRESSING ANGER
- ANGER IS DANGEROUS AND BAD.
- EXPLODE IN ANGER TO MAKE A POINT.
- SARCASM IS AN ACCEPTABLE WAY TO RELEASE ANGER.

6. FAMILY
- YOU OWE YOUR PARENTS FOR ALL THEY'VE DONE FOR YOU.
- DON'T SPEAK OF YOUR FAMILY'S "DIRTY LAUNDRY" IN PUBLIC.
- DUTY TO FAMILY AND CULTURE COMES BEFORE EVERYTHING.

7. RELATIONSHIPS
- DON'T TRUST PEOPLE. THEY WILL LET YOU DOWN.
- DON'T EVER LET ANYONE HURT YOU.
- DON'T SHOW VULNERABILITY.

8. ATTITUDES TOWARD OTHER CULTURES
- ONLY BE CLOSE FRIENDS WITH PEOPLE WHO ARE LIKE YOU.
- DO NOT MARRY A PERSON OF ANOTHER RACE OR CULTURE.
- CERTAIN CULTURES/RACES ARE NOT AS GOOD AS OURS.

9. SUCCESS
- IS GETTING INTO THE "BEST SCHOOLS."
- IS MAKING LOTS OF MONEY.
- IS GETTING MARRIED AND HAVING CHILDREN.

10. FEELINGS AND EMOTIONS
- YOU ARE NOT ALLOWED TO HAVE CERTAIN FEELINGS.
- YOUR FEELINGS ARE NOT IMPORTANT.
- REACTING WITH YOUR FEELINGS WITHOUT THINKING IS OKAY.

(❙❙) *Pause the Video*

Workbook Activities (20 minutes)

Individual Activity (7 minutes)

1. Read the "Unbiblical Family Commandments" on page 67. Circle the two or three commandments that you think have most negatively impacted you.

2. Choose one commandment that you would most like to change. Put a star next to it. Note: For a sample of biblical family commandments, see Appendix B (page 170).

Small Group Sharing (13 minutes)

In groups of three or four, reflect on these two experiences (the Genogram and Unbiblical Family Commandments) and individually complete this sentence: *I am beginning to realize . . .*

(▶) VIDEO: Closing Summary (4 minutes)

Video Notes

Observe your behavior over the next week. When something seems out of order ask yourself, "How did my family do that?"

As you prayerfully reflect on your genogram in this coming week, remember:

- Joseph had a family history of pain, loss, and tragedy (see Genesis 37–50). He could have said, "My life is ruined. My family wrecked me." But he did not.
- God, in his sovereignty, put you in your family as he put Joseph in his.
- God works "in, through, and in spite" of your past—even the very worst—in hidden and mysterious ways.

- God wants to take your past and give you a great future out of it. May you trust God to take all the broken parts of your history and create something beautiful with your life that you can offer to the world.

Optional Session Wrap-up (5 minutes)

Together with your small group, ask any questions of clarification regarding this session and then briefly close in prayer.

PERSONAL ACTION STEPS

- Review your genogram at least once during the next week, asking the Holy Spirit to show you other insights he might have for you. When will you do that?
- If appropriate, meet with a trusted friend to share insights from your genogram. With whom? When?
- Before the next session, practice the Community Temperature Reading, Stop Mind Reading, and Clarify Expectations skills at least one time.

Between-Sessions Personal Study
Session Three

Read the pre-session assignment for Session 4 on pages 76–78. Use the space provided to note any insights or questions you might want to bring to the next group session.

Prayerfully read Week 3 of the *Emotionally Healthy Relationships Day by Day* devotional, "Genogram Your Family." Use the space provided to answer the Questions to Consider and/or to journal your thoughts each day.

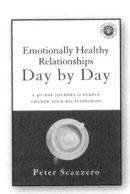

DAY 1 Questions to Consider:

What darkness—setback, failure, disappointment, suffering, mistake—first comes to mind when you think about your past? How might God want to reveal himself to you as you surrender to him the pain of your past?

How might God be transforming you through the pain and losses of your past?

DAY 2 Questions to Consider:

How might a present limit or past failure be God's gift of love for you, and a gift you can give to the world?

How might you hold on to God when he is silent and you don't "feel his presence"?

DAY 3   Questions to Consider:

What first comes to mind when you think about an unhealthy message that was communicated by silence in your family of origin? How do you sense Jesus may be inviting you to unlearn that message in order to live in a healthier way in God's family?

How might God be doing an important but unseen work in, through, and in spite of any hiddenness you are experiencing right now?

DAY 4   Questions to Consider:

What is one specific area in your life that God is inviting you to patiently trust him today?

What hopes and dreams come to mind when you consider that God wastes nothing?

DAY 5 Questions to Consider:

How is God inviting you to trust him today?

Name one area in your life where you are curious of what God might be doing—especially as it relates to your family of origin history. How might he be inviting you to wait patiently for him?

Explore the Iceberg

Session Four

PRE-SESSION READING

Jesus had a full sense of what he was about. On the evening before his arrest, he took the role of a slave and began washing the twelve disciples' feet, even Judas's. The apostle John notes, "Jesus knew that the Father had put all things under his power, and that he had come from God and was returning to God" (John 13:3). He was deeply aware of who he was and what he was doing. This enabled him to break from the expectations of his family, friends, disciples, and wider religious culture and to follow God's unique plan for his life. In the same way, a deep awareness of what we are feeling and doing gives us the courage to begin doing life differently (and hopefully more in line with God's will) and developing new, healthier relational patterns.

Scripture portrays Jesus as one who had intense, raw, emotional experiences and was able to express his emotions in unashamed, unembarrassed freedom to others. He did not repress or project his feelings onto others. Instead, we read of Jesus responsibly experiencing the full range of human emotion throughout his earthly ministry. In today's language, he would be considered *emotionally intelligent*, a term popularized by Daniel Goleman today.[1] . . .

Some of us feel that it's greedy and selfish to pay attention to what we are feeling and doing. In my early years as a Christian, I heard few, if any, discussions about the awareness of feelings as one key to discipleship. There are many other important issues related to maturing in Christ, but an honest examination of our emotions and feelings is central. This inward look is not to encourage a self-absorbed introspection that feeds narcissism. The ultimate purpose is to allow the gospel to transform all of you—both above and below the iceberg. The end result will be that you and I will be better lovers of God and other people.

Without doing the work of becoming aware of your feelings and actions, along with their impact on others, it is scarcely possible to enter deeply into the life experiences of other people. How can you enter someone else's world when you have not entered your own?

When I read the story of Job's ranting before God, Jeremiah's anguish about God's word burning in his heart "like a fire" (Jeremiah 20:9), Moses' struggles in the wilderness, or David's anguish of feeling abandoned by God, I observe leaders of God in the brutal, painful honesty of wrestling with emotions, feelings, and the realities going on around them. That's why their life stories speak to us so powerfully. . . .

In meeting the Samaritan woman at the well (John 4), Jesus consistently confronted her with the "why" question. He went below the surface of her actions to wrestle with bigger life-related questions: Why are you at the well in the middle of the day? Because you are ashamed? Why are you running from husband to husband? What void are you trying to fill?

She attempted to sidetrack the conversation, keeping it above the surface. So she asked Jesus about the best place to worship (John 4:20). Jesus, instead, called her to examine her life beneath the surface of the iceberg and consider her immoral lifestyle as an indication of her insatiable thirst for love.

Jesus also pointed others to "why" questions. He once corrected the Pharisees and teachers of the law, who were passionate about external behavior issues but were not doing the difficult work on their insides. "Listen to me, everyone, and understand this. Nothing outside you can defile you by going into you. Rather, it is what comes out of you that defiles you" (Mark 7:14–15). Jesus tried to reorient them to the "why's" of their behavior, to their motivations, and to their hearts (7:21).

Once I begin to be aware of what I am doing, how I am feeling, and how it is impacting others, I need to ask myself the difficult "why" question. For example:

- Why am I always in a hurry? Why am I so impatient?
- What am I so anxious? . . .
- Why do I dread this meeting today at 2:00 p.m.? Why am I so flooded with fear? . . .
- Why do I avoid certain people?
- Why do I have a need to immediately return all phone calls and emails? Or why do I avoid returning certain phone calls, emails, or text messages? Is it because I want to please people?

Wrestling with these types of probing questions about the depths of our hearts is, to say the least, an uncomfortable experience!

In the past I spent hours with God, beseeching him to accomplish my agenda and plans. However, now I spend much more time with God, praying for His will to be done, not my own. And I rest in his love, wrestling with the "why" questions in an open, receptive way before him.

It takes courage to ask myself: What am I really feeling in this situation? What might be going on here? King Saul was unaware of what was going on inside of him. His "doing" for God did not flow from his "being" with God. We see him repeatedly blind to his jealousy, fear, hatred and anger. Unlike David, we don't observe Saul cultivating his relationship with God. Eventually, his life choices destroy him (see 1 Samuel 17–31).

Blaise Pascal wrote: "All men's miseries derive from not being able to sit in a quiet room alone."[2] This involves taking my feelings and thoughts about why I am feeling this way and bringing them honestly to God. I ask, "What does this represent? What might you, God, be saying to me? What do I learn about myself in this? About life? About other people?"

— *The Emotionally Healthy Church*, Updated and Expanded, pages 78, 81–83

GROUP MEETING

Daily Office (10 minutes)

Do one of the Daily Offices from Week 4 of *Emotionally Healthy Relationships Day by Day* to begin your session.

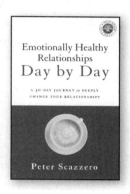

Introduction (2 minutes)

As the accompanying image illustrates, about 10 percent of an iceberg is visible at the surface, representing the part of our lives that people see. It can also represent the part of our lives that we are consciously aware of.

The *Titanic* sank because it collided with a section of the submerged 90 percent of an iceberg. Most people shipwreck, or live inconsistent lives, because of forces and motivations beneath the surface of their lives that they have never considered.

Iceberg Model
What Lies Beneath the Surface

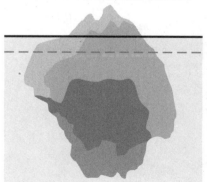

Solomon said it well in Proverbs 4:23, "Above all else, guard your heart, for everything you do flows from it." Scripture portrays Jesus as deeply aware of who he is and what he is feeling. We read of him responsibly experiencing the full range of human emotions throughout his earthly ministry. This contributed to his faithfulness in following the Father's unique plan for his life, and his breaking away from the expectations of his family, friends, disciples, and the crowds.

Growing Connected (10 minutes)

1. *Day by Day* Debrief: Being still to know God more deeply (Psalm 46:10) is an invitation to surrender our will to God's will, as well as resting from our strivings and fears. How might silence enable you to surrender, relax, and enjoy God's rest in the midst of the anxieties you carry today?

2. Turn to the person next to you and share on a scale of 1 to 5, with 5 being the highest, how you would rate your awareness of what is going on inside of you.

Bible Study (10 minutes)

1. Read aloud Psalm 22:1–2, 12–14 (below). Try to put yourself in David's shoes (and in Jesus' place, as these verses also refer prophetically to his death on the cross). Name a few of the emotions David may have been feeling as he wrote this psalm.

> My God, my God, why have you forsaken me?
> > Why are you so far from saving me,
> > so far from my cries of anguish?
> My God, I cry out by day, but you do not answer,
> > by night, but I find no rest.
> Many bulls surround me;
> > strong bulls of Bashan encircle me.
> Roaring lions that tear their prey
> > open their mouths wide against me.
> I am poured out like water,
> > and all my bones are out of joint.
> My heart has turned to wax;
> > it has melted within me.

2. If David visited your church and shared what he wrote in this text, how might you respond?

▶ VIDEO: Explore the Iceberg (13 minutes)

Video Notes
What Does It Mean to Explore the Iceberg?[3]

The purpose: To become aware of your emotions, with the goal of processing them and discerning God's will.

Scripture teaches that feelings are a key part of what it means to be a human being made in God's image. For example:
- David
- Job
- Jeremiah
- Jesus

Human beings are like icebergs: 10 percent is above the surface and visible; 90 percent is below the surface and invisible.

Example of Franklin Delano Roosevelt

Three Truths about Emotions
1. Unprocessed emotions don't die.
2. Healthy community requires that people know themselves.
3. Feelings help us discern God's voice.

Ask yourself: *How is God coming to me through how I'm feeling?*

�II *Pause the Video*

Workbook Activities (20 minutes)

Individual Activity (10 minutes)

Read the following instructions aloud before beginning:

1. Four questions will be read aloud and you will be given two minutes per question to write your answers in the spaces provided on following pages.
2. Write as many responses as come to mind. Draw from the present, recent past, or distant past.
3. For some of you, this will flow easily and time will go quickly. For others, it may be difficult and uncomfortable. We invite you to do this before the Lord as a spiritual practice of prayer, letting God guide you. If you finish before the allotted time frame ends, don't be afraid of the silence. Be open to anything else God may want to bring to the surface.
4. You may want to begin each of the four questions by closing your eyes for a few moments before you start writing.

What are you angry about (from the past or present)?

What are you sad about (e.g., a small or big loss, disappointment, or choice)?

What are you anxious about (e.g., your money, future, family, health, job)?

What are you glad about (e.g., a relationship, an opportunity, your church)?

Small Group Sharing (15 minutes)

In groups of three or four:

1. What was the individual activity like for you? What did you learn?

2. How did the family you grew up in express anger, sadness, or fear?

3. How do you deal with your anger, sadness, or fear today?

▶ VIDEO: Closing Summary (6 minutes)

Video Notes

Final Reminders

1. Difficult emotions that go unprocessed cover over pleasurable feelings.
2. If we don't process our emotions, we end up leaking them and often not taking responsibility for them.
3. Anger is often a surface emotion.

Look at what is behind the anger and ask yourself two questions:

*   What am I afraid of?
*   What am I hurt or sad about?

Final Encouragements

- Do Explore the Iceberg at least twice the next week.
- Consider doing an Explore the Iceberg aloud with a safe friend. Have them ask you the four questions from the Individual Activity.
- Pray the Psalms.

Optional Session Wrap-up (5 minutes)

Together with your small group, ask any questions of clarification regarding this session and then briefly close in prayer.

PERSONAL ACTION STEP

Practice the Explore the Iceberg skill at least once per week, either alone, in a journal, or aloud with a trusted friend.

I plan on practicing the Explore the Iceberg skill:

With whom? _____

When? _____

Between-Sessions Personal Study
Session Four

Read the pre-session assignment for Session 5 on pages 92–94. Use the space provided to note any insights or questions you might want to bring to the next group session.

Prayerfully read Week 4 of the *Emotionally Healthy Relationships Day by Day* devotional, "Explore the Iceberg." Use the space provided to answer the Questions to Consider and/or to journal your thoughts each day.

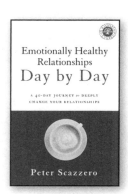

DAY 1 Questions to Consider:

In light of Jesus' ability to express his feelings to his closest friends, how would you describe your ability to do the same? Do you do so easily, awkwardly, with great difficulty, or never?

In what ways do you tend to suppress or deny difficult emotions—anger, sadness, fear— rather than admit them to yourself and God?

DAY 2 Questions to Consider:

Growing up, what messages did you pick up from your family about anger, sadness, and fear? How have those messages impacted you as an adult?

How might God be inviting you to be still today so that you may be more aware of your feelings and better hear his voice?

DAY 3 Questions to Consider:

How might your prayer life change if, like David, you could bring to God what is actually in you and not what you think should be in you?

As you consider your fears today, do Jesus' words, "Don't be afraid," come across as critical or comforting? Why?

DAY 4 Questions to Consider:

Take a moment to think back over the last twenty-four hours. What "ordinary and small gifts" did God entrust to you for which you can be thankful?

Briefly reflect on the events and interactions of your last twenty-four hours. Then ask yourself: When did I experience joy, peace, increased energy, or a sense of God's presence (consolation)? And when did I experience sadness, apathy, energy draining out of me, or a sense of God's absence (desolation)?

DAY 5 Questions to Consider:

As you reflect on any current or recent experiences of anger, how would you describe the "warning indicator light" or the message your anger might be trying to send you?

Which line in Richard Rohr's prayer do you identify with most? Why?

Listen Incarnationally

Session Five

PRE-SESSION READING

The fruit of a mature spirituality is to be an incarnational presence to another person. It was for Jesus. It is, I believe, for all his followers. . . .

When is the last time someone said to you, "Let me tell you about those Christians—they are fantastic listeners! I have never seen a group of people more interested to know my world, curious, asking questions—listening to me!" . . .

Give yourself this little listening test. Circle all the statements you can affirm.

1. My close friends would describe me as a responsive listener.
2. When people are upset with me, I am able to listen to them without being defensive.
3. I listen not only to the words people say but also to the feelings behind their words and their body language.
4. I have little interest in judging other people or quickly giving my opinion to them.
5. I am able to validate another person's feelings with empathy.
6. I am aware of my defensive mechanisms in stressful conversations (e.g. appeasing, ignoring, blaming, distracting).
7. I am profoundly aware of how the family I was raised in has shaped my present listening style.
8. I ask for clarification when listening rather than "fill in the blanks" or make assumptions.
9. I don't interrupt to get my point across when another is speaking.
10. I give people my undivided attention when they are talking to me.

If you circled 8–10 statements, you are an outstanding listener; if you circled 6–7, you are very good; 4–5, good; 3 or fewer, poor—"you are in trouble." If you want to be really brave, after you score yourself, ask your spouse or someone close to you to rate you as a listener. You may be surprised. . . .

The great challenge in incarnation, for most of us, is to hold on to ourselves and not to lose ourselves when we enter another person's world. To do so is to be like Jesus. The apostle John records that prior to Jesus' washing his disciples' feet, he "knew that the Father had put all things under his power, and that he had come from God and was returning to God" (John 13:3). Jesus never ceased to be God when he took on human flesh and became one of us.

At New Life, we have people from over seventy-three different countries. Almost one-fourth are African American and West Indian. Another third are Asian (Chinese, Korean, Indonesian, Filipino, etc.). The rest are Hispanic, Jewish, Eastern European, African and Anglo. I am a second-generation Italian-American. While I am called to go into other people's worlds, it is necessary that I do not lose my God-given self in the process.

In order to be an emotionally and spiritually mature disciple of Jesus, this is perhaps the most difficult, challenging principle to apply. Without this, you end up a chameleon like Leonard Zelig.

Woody Allen, in his movie *Zelig*, traces the life of a human chameleon named Leonard Zelig. He becomes a celebrity in the 1920s due to his unique power and ability to look and act like whoever is around him—Black, Indian, obese, Chinese, Scottish—you name it, and Zelig becomes it. This human chameleon has no identity or "self" of his own. He becomes whomever he is around. He jokes with prizefighter Jack Dempsey. He is with Hitler on the speaker's platform at Nuremberg.

Zelig assumes whatever strong personalities he meets up with. With the Chinese he is straight out of China. With rabbis, he miraculously grows a beard and side curls. With psychiatrists, he repeats their jargon and strokes his chin as if he were a wise man. At the Vatican he is part of Pope Pius XI's clerical attendants. As a chameleon, he changes color, accent, and shape as the world around him changes. Everywhere he simply conforms. He wants only to be safe, to fit in, to be accepted, to be liked. He is famous for being nobody, a nonperson.[1]

At times we empathize *too* much. Out of fear we (sometimes) do not assert our preferences and point of view. And we lose ourselves in the process. Remember, Jesus is our model. He became fully man, but he remained fully God. . . .

At the same time, Jesus also hung between two worlds: heaven and earth. Life would have been much simpler for Jesus if he stayed in heaven with the Father. This world, for Jesus, was not safe. But by entering our world, he invited sorrow and pain into his life. He was misunderstood and not appreciated. He died a naked, lonely death on a cross, hanging literally between heaven and earth.

It was, in a word, messy.

Jesus said, "Students are not above their teacher, nor servants above their master" (Matthew 10:24). You and I may not die literally on a cross as Jesus did, but we will die in other ways when we incarnate. It costs time, energy, and, almost always, a disruption to our risk-free world.

When we choose to incarnate, we hang between our own world and the world of another person. We are called to remain faithful to who we are, not losing our essence, while at the same time entering into the world of another. We can be assured, however, that as Jesus' incarnation and death brought great life, so our choice to do the same will also result in resurrection life and much fruit in us and others.

—Adapted from *The Emotionally Healthy Church*, pages 189, 190, 193–194, 196

GROUP MEETING

Daily Office (10 minutes)

Do one of the Daily Offices from Week 5 of *Emotionally Healthy Relationships Day by Day* to begin your session.

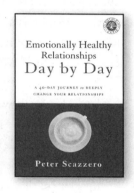

Introduction (2 minutes)

The Gospels are filled with accounts of Jesus' interactions with individuals: Matthew, Nathaniel, Nicodemus, a Samaritan woman, Zacchaeus, and many others. When the rich young ruler came up to him, for example, Jesus "looked at him and loved him" (Mark 10:21). He listened. He was present, never distracted or in a rush. He took the time to explore their stories.

Many of us have heard sermons about the need to listen well and to be slow to speak (see Proverbs 17:27–28; James 1:19). But listening does not come naturally to anyone. David Augsburger notes that listening is so closely linked to loving that the two are almost indistinguishable. Most of us did not learn to be good listeners while growing up in our families, but it is a crucial skill that can be learned. It remains one of the most significant ways we can practically demonstrate our love for one another.

Growing Connected (10 minutes)

1. *Day by Day* Debrief: Through silence and stillness, God invites us to open our hearts to receive his unwavering love. On a scale of 1 to 5 (1 being the lowest and 5 the highest), where would you place your experience with silence as a means to receive God's love?

2. Turn to the person next to you and share (in a few words) a time when you felt listened to. What did the other person do that caused you to feel heard?

Bible Study (10 minutes)

God entered our planet and forever changed it. God became incarnate, taking on human flesh. He knew there was no better way to show human beings his love than by fully entering our lives. Jesus modeled incarnational love when he entered our world and walked in our shoes. Read aloud John 1:1–3, 14.

> In the beginning was the Word, and the Word was with God, and the Word was God. He was with God in the beginning. Through him all things were made; without him nothing was made that has been made.
>
> The Word became flesh and made his dwelling among us. We have seen his glory, the glory of the one and only Son, who came from the Father, full of grace and truth.

1. Step into Jesus' shoes. What feelings might he have experienced in leaving heaven and entering a world so different from heaven?

2. Describe a time when you left your "world" and entered one very different from your own.

▶ VIDEO: Listen Incarnationally (20 minutes)

Video Notes
Introduction

What does it mean to Listen Incarnationally?

The purpose: To listen at a heart level with empathy, attuned to the words and nonverbal communication of another person (i.e., so that the other person feels felt by you).

"Being heard is so close to being loved that for the average person they are almost indistinguishable." —David Augsburger

"From experience, you know that those who care for you become present to you. When they listen, they listen to you. When they speak, you know they speak to you. . . . Their presence is a healing presence because they accept you on your terms, and they encourage you to take your own life seriously." —Henri Nouwen

Speaking

How did the family you grew up in speak to one another?

We speak differently in the new family of Jesus. We speak:
1. Respectfully

2. Honestly

3. Clearly

4. Timely

In the last few days, when has your speech *not* been respectful, honest, clear, or timely? Imagine how you might have done that interaction differently.

Listening

In unhealthy togetherness, we want or expect another person to think and feel the way we do.

In healthy togetherness, the individuals respect each other's separateness, allowing the other to have their own thoughts, feelings, fears, and values.

Attunement—not just listening to words but the nonverbal communication (e.g., facial expressions, tone of voice, tears, body posture, intensity of words).
- The person feels "felt" by the listener.
- The prize is emotional connection, not information.

Jesus serves as a beautiful model of listening:
1. Jesus left his world. (When we listen, we leave our world.)
2. He entered our world. (We enter another's world through listening.)
3. He held on to himself. (When we listen, we don't have to agree.)
4. Jesus hung between two worlds. (I may not like what I hear, but I can hang between the tension of our different perspectives.)

Incarnational Listening: The Wrong Way

Incarnational Listening: The Right Way

Keep in mind:
- Incarnational Listening might look wooden, but it has a purpose.
- Listening does not mean agreement.
- Notice the listener doesn't get defensive or take things personally.

Guidelines for the Listener and the Speaker

As the Listener:
- Give the speaker your full attention.

- Step into the speaker's shoes and feel what they are feeling.
- Avoid judging or interpreting.
- Reflect back as accurately as you can what you heard them say.
- When you think the speaker is done, ask, "Is there more?"
- When the speaker is done, ask, "Of everything you have shared, what is the most important thing you want me to remember?"

As the Speaker:
- Speak in the "I."
- Keep your statements brief.
- Stop to let the listener paraphrase.
- Include your feelings. (For a list of feeling words, see Appendix C, page 171.)
- Be honest, clear, and respectful.
- It is critically important to help people distinguish a thought from a feeling.

In our culture, we often say "I feel that . . ." to share a thought or opinion. A key principle to remember is when the word *that* follows "I feel," what's being shared is not a feeling but an opinion or a thought. To use the phrase "I feel" correctly, it needs to be followed by a feeling (e.g., "I am . . . sad, disappointed, anxious, happy, etc."). We are not able to get beneath the iceberg without sharing feelings.

> e.g., "I feel that this supermarket's prices are too high." What you are really saying is: "I think (or I believe) that the supermarket's prices are too high."

> If there were feelings behind it, it might sound like this: "I really like this supermarket, but I feel sad that I can't afford to shop there."

(II) *Pause the Video*

Workbook Activities (30 minutes)

Partner Activity (20 minutes)

1. Pair up with one other person. Spread out as much as possible in the room.

2. Face each other and decide who will go first. Allow seven minutes for each person. Remember: This is designed to be a "win-win" exercise. As the speaker shares honestly and respectfully, your goal is to listen to your partner with understanding, respect, and empathy.

3. Each person will respond to the following questions:

    - **What is the biggest thing impacting you right now? and how are you feeling about it?** (If you are with someone you know, please don't make your sharing about them.)

    As the Speaker, remember to:
    - Speak in the "I."
    - Keep your statements brief.
    - Stop to let the listener paraphrase.
    - Include your feelings (see page 171).
    - Remember: Be honest, clear, and respectful.

    As the Listener, remember to:
    - Give the speaker your full attention. Don't think about your rebuttal.
    - Step into the speaker's shoes—feel what he/she is feeling.
    - Avoid judging or interpreting.
    - Reflect back as accurately as you can what you heard the speaker say.
    - Ask, "Is there more?" when you think he/she is done.
    - Finally, ask, "Of everything you have shared, what is the most important thing you want me to remember?"

Small Group Sharing (15 minutes)

In groups of three or four:

1. What was the experience like for you as the speaker? The listener?

2. How was your family of origin at listening? Speaking?

3. Name one or two obstacles you will need to overcome to grow into a person who listens well.

▶ VIDEO: Closing Summary (4 minutes)

Video Notes

These guidelines to listen incarnationally are meant to be like the training wheels of a bicycle. The structure is necessary, especially in the beginning, to break deeply embedded bad habits.

This is a great tool to mature us into greater character and maturity—especially when the other person is saying something difficult to hear.

This is not a problem-solving skill. That will come in the final skill—Fighting Cleanly.

Optional Session Wrap-up (5 minutes)

Together with your small group, ask any questions of clarification regarding this session and then briefly close in prayer.

PERSONAL ACTION STEP

Practice the Listening Incarnationally skill once or twice before the next session.

I plan on practicing the Listening Incarnationally skill:

With whom? _____

When? _____

Between-Sessions Personal Study
Session Five

Read the pre-session assignment for Session 6 on pages 110–113. Use the space provided to note any insights or questions you might want to bring to the next group session.

Prayerfully read Week 5 of the *Emotionally Healthy Relationships Day by Day* devotional, "Listen Incarnationally." Use the space provided to answer the Questions to Consider and/or to journal your thoughts each day.

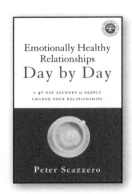

DAY 1 Questions to Consider:

What phrases or sentences from the Mother Teresa quotes most speak to you today?

Recognizing that "a person blossoms when undergoing the experience of being loved," who is one person you can help to blossom this week by intentionally offering them the experience of being loved?

DAY 2 Questions to Consider:

What would you say is your greatest obstacle or challenge to being fully present and engaged with others?

In what way(s) are you tempted to be distracted when you are with people rather than be present, deeply listening and accepting them on their own terms?

DAY 3 Questions to Consider:

What adjustments might you need to make to treat each person you meet today as a "Thou" rather than an "It"?

What might be one practical way you can slow down in order to love someone in the next twenty-four hours?

DAY 4 Questions to Consider:

With whom might God be inviting you to be a more humble, attentive listener today?

As you anticipate spending time with someone today, what difference might it make in your ability to listen well if you could imagine holding that person like a small bird in the palm of your hands?

DAY 5   Questions to Consider:

Jesus acknowledged a promise when he said, "Did I not tell you that if you believe, you will see the glory of God?" How might this promise encourage you to step over your fears and listen to the pain of others today?

What is one practical step you can take today to lessen your distractibility and offer a deeper, more sustained focus to God and to the people around you?

Climb the Ladder of Integrity

Session Six

PRE-SESSION READING

Living your God-given life involves remaining faithful to your true self. It entails distinguishing your true self from the demands and voices around you and discerning the unique vision, calling, and mission the Father has given to you.[1] It requires listening to God from within yourself and understanding how he has uniquely made you. Knowing your personality, temperament, likes and dislikes, thoughts, and feelings all contribute to your discovery. . . .

It seemed that almost everyone had expectations, or a false self, to impose on Jesus' life. In living faithfully to his true self, he disappointed a lot of people. Jesus was secure in his Father's love, in himself, and thus was able to withstand enormous pressure. He left his family of origin and their expectations of a carpenter's son and became an inner-directed, separate adult. As a result, he disappointed his family. At one point, his mother and siblings wondered if he was out of his mind (Mark 3:21).

He disappointed the people he grew up with in Nazareth. When Jesus declared who he really was as the Messiah, they tried to push him off a cliff (Luke 4:28–29). He remained self-assured in his beliefs, regardless of the outrage of the crowds in his hometown.

He disappointed his closest friends, the twelve disciples. They projected onto Jesus their own picture of the kind of Messiah Jesus was to be. This did not include a shameful end to his life. They quit on him. Judas, one of his closest friends, "stabbed him in the back" for being true to himself. But even though they misunderstood him, Jesus never held it against them.

Jesus listened without reacting. He communicated without antagonizing. Yet he deeply disappointed the crowds. They wanted an earthly Messiah who would feed them, fix all their problems, overthrow the Roman oppressors, work miracles, and give inspiring sermons. Somehow Christ was able to serve and love them, again, without holding it against them.

He disappointed the religious leaders. They did not appreciate the disruption his presence brought to their day-to-day lives or to their theology. They finally attributed his power to demons. Nonetheless, Jesus was able to maintain a non-anxious presence in the midst of great stress.

Jesus was not *selfless*. He did not live as if *only* other people counted. He knew his value and worth. He had friends. He asked people to help him. At the same time Jesus was not *selfish*. He did not live as if nobody else counted. He gave his life out of love for others. From a place of loving union with his Father, Jesus had a mature, healthy "true self."

The pressure on us to live a life that is not our own is also great. Powerful generational forces and spiritual warfare work against us. Yet living faithfully to our true self in Christ represents one of the great tasks of discipleship.

One very helpful way to clarify this process of growing in our faithfulness to our true selves in a new way is through the use of a new term: *differentiation*. Developed by Murray Bowen, the founder of modern family systems theory, it refers to a person's capacity to "define his or her own life's goals and values apart from the pressures of those around them."[2] The key emphasis of differentiation is on the ability to think clearly and carefully as another means, besides our feelings, of knowing ourselves.

Differentiation involves the ability to hold on to who you are and who you are not. The degree to which you are able to affirm your distinct values and goals apart from the pressures around you (separateness) while remaining close to people important to you (togetherness) helps determine your level of differentiation. People with a high level of differentiation have their own beliefs, convictions, directions, goals, and values apart from the pressures around them. They can choose, before God, how they want to be without being controlled by the approval or disapproval of others. Intensity of feelings, high stress, or the anxiety of others around them does not overwhelm their capacity to think rationally.

I may not agree with you or you with me. Yet I can remain in relationship with you. I don't have to detach from you, reject you, avoid you, or criticize you to validate myself. I can be myself apart from you.

Read through my adaptation of Bowen's scale of differentiation beginning below. On the lower end of the scale are those with little sense of their unique God-given life. They need continual affirmation and validation from others because they don't have a clear sense of who they are. They depend on what other people think and feel in order to have a sense of their own worth and identity. Or out of fear of getting too close to someone and thus swallowed up, they may avoid closeness to others completely. Under stress they have little ability to distinguish between their feelings and their thought (intellectual) process.

Considering that Jesus was 100 percent true to himself, or "self-differentiated," where might you place yourself on this scale?

0. . . . . 25. . . . . 50. . . . . 75. 100

0–25

- Can't distinguish between fact and feeling
- Emotionally needy and highly reactive to others
- Much of life energy spent in winning the approval of others
- Little energy for goal-directed activities
- Can't say, "I think . . . I believe . . ."
- Little emotional separation from their families
- Dependent marital relationships
- Do very poorly in transitions, crises, and life adjustments
- Unable to see where they end and others begin

25–50

- Some ability to distinguish between fact and feeling
- Most of self is a "false self" and reflected from others
- When anxiety is low, they function relatively well
- Quick to imitate others and change themselves to gain acceptance from others
- Often talk one set of principles/beliefs, yet do another
- Self-esteem soars with compliments or is crushed by criticism
- Become anxious (i.e., highly reactive and "freaking out") when a relationship system falls apart or becomes unbalanced
- Often make poor decisions due to their inability to think clearly under stress
- Seek power, honor, knowledge, and love from others to clothe their false selves

50–75

- Aware of the thinking and feeling functions that work as a team
- Reasonable level of "true self"
- Can follow life goals that are determined from within
- Can state beliefs calmly without putting others down
- Marriage is a functioning partnership where intimacy can be enjoyed without losing the self
- Can allow children to progress through developmental phases into adult autonomy
- Function well—alone or with others
- Able to cope with crises without falling apart
- Stay in relational connection with others without insisting they see the world the same

75–100

(Few people function at this level)

- Are principle oriented and goal directed—secure in who they are, unaffected by criticism or praise
- Are able to leave family of origin and become an inner-directed, separate adult
- Sure of their beliefs but not dogmatic or closed in their thinking
- Can hear and evaluate beliefs of others, discarding old beliefs in favor of new ones
- Can listen without reacting and communicate without antagonizing others
- Can respect others without having to change them
- Aware of dependence on others and responsibility *for* others
- Free to enjoy life and play
- Able to maintain a non-anxious presence in the midst of stress and pressure
- Able to take responsibility for their own destiny

—*Emotionally Healthy Spirituality*, Updated Edition, pages 56–61

GROUP MEETING

Daily Office (10 minutes)

Do one of the Daily Offices from Week 6 of *Emotionally Healthy Relationships Day by Day* to begin your session.

Introduction (2 minutes)

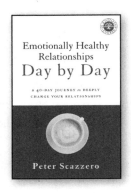

God has shaped and crafted us internally—each with our own personality, thoughts, dreams, temperament, feelings, talents, gifts, and desires. He has planted "true seeds of self" inside of us, inviting us to listen to him and live faithfully to our true selves in Christ.

Secure in his Father's love, Jesus lived with integrity. Despite enormous pressure to live according to the expectations and plans of others, he remained faithful to the Father's will for his life.

We violate our integrity when we do not live what we believe, think, or feel, or when we ignore values we hold dear. Often who we are "on stage" (i.e., in front of others) slowly becomes different from who we are "off stage" (i.e., when we are alone).

Something dies inside of us when we fail to speak up about our values and preferences. God invites us to ground our identity in an ongoing experience of the love of God in Christ and respectfully assert ourselves.

Growing Connected (10 minutes)

1. *Day by Day* Debrief: Throughout church history, it has often been noted that silence is God's first language. When we are silent, we make room to hear God speak. In what new ways are you beginning to hear God through your silence and the Day by Day readings?

2. Turn to the person next to you and name one specific fear you carry that keeps you from having a difficult conversation with a friend, boss, coworker, or family member.

Bible Study (10 minutes)

When the apostle Peter first came to Antioch from Jerusalem, he welcomed and ate with uncircumcised Gentile Christians. Later, a group of Jewish Christians arrived and convinced Peter to withdraw and separate from those Gentiles. They convinced Peter it was against God's will to eat with the uncircumcised and "unclean" Gentiles. Read Galatians 2:11–14, the apostle Paul's account of this situation.

> When Cephas [Peter] came to Antioch, I [Paul] opposed him to his face, because he stood condemned. For before certain men came from James, he used to eat with the Gentiles. But when they arrived, he began to draw back and separate himself from the Gentiles because he was afraid of those who belonged to the circumcision group. The other Jews joined him in his hypocrisy, so that by their hypocrisy even Barnabas was led astray.
>
> When I saw that they were not acting in line with the truth of the gospel, I said to Cephas in front of them all, "You are a Jew, yet you live like a Gentile and not like a Jew. How is it, then, that you force Gentiles to follow Jewish customs?

1. Why, according to Paul, did Peter separate himself from the Gentiles?

2. What did Paul risk in speaking to Peter? What might have gotten lost if Paul had not gone to Peter?

3. In what area(s) of your life might you be avoiding a difficult conversation or acting in a way that is inconsistent to your values?

VIDEO: Climb the Ladder of Integrity (17 minutes)

▶ *Video Notes*

The Climb the Ladder of Integrity skill is used when something is bothering you, but you can't quite get a handle on what it is; when you are frustrated, angry, or hurt, it's a cue that something important to you may have been violated.

The purpose: To clarify your values by processing your thoughts and feelings (and, if appropriate, to assert yourself respectfully).

The Ladder of Integrity

- Helps you get honest and clear about what is going on inside of you.
- Helps you uncover and clarify your values so that you can assert yourself with the other person (if that is appropriate).
- Is important because Scripture tells us each of us is created in God's image with distinct preferences, hopes, dreams, and values. Climbing the Ladder of Integrity may sometimes involve moral issues of right and wrong. Other times it may involve gray areas or personal preferences.

    e.g., Galatians 2 (Peter and Paul's conflict over the gospel)

    e.g., Romans 14 (examples of gray areas and different preferences)

Important Reminder: This Is Not a Conflict Resolution Tool!

- It is for getting clear within yourself so you can identify your values and then, if appropriate, respectfully share them.
- Note the progression in the Ladder (see page 117)
    - Thoughts and Feelings (1–6)
    - Values (7–10)
    - Hopes (11–12)

Model Climbing the Ladder of Integrity (Phil)

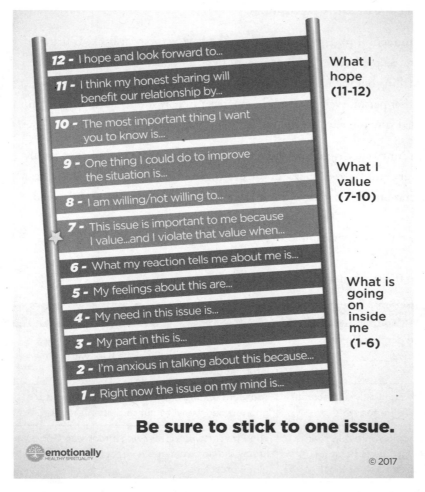

Pause the Video

Workbook Activities (30 minutes)

Individual Activity (4 minutes)

1. Identify a nonvolatile issue that is bothering you (e.g., someone's lateness, cell phone usage, driving, messiness, TV/computer usage, texting during a meal, your family's holiday plans, lack of honesty, missing meetings).

Note: Before you start, make sure that your issue is not because of faulty assumptions or a failure to clarify expectations.

e.g., You sent three emails to someone and have yet to hear back. You are so frustrated and bothered that you want to do a Ladder about it. Before you start filling out the Ladder, however, check out your assumption to be sure the other person even received the emails! You may simply need to say, "I'm puzzled why you have not responded to my emails."

e.g., Your twenty-eight-year-old son and his girlfriend do not join the family for every Sunday at dinner and you are angry. It may just be that you have an expectation of them that is not realistic and to which they have not agreed.

2. Write down the issue by completing the following sentence stem:

Right now the issue on my mind is . . .

UNCLEAR (the wrong way)	CLEAR (the right way)
1. You are demanding and insensitive.	On my second day at work, you emailed me a 2-sentence request to make a flyer with little information and without talking to me.
2. You are highligly distractable when we are together.	You were texting and checking emails on your phone when we were out to dinner last week.
3. The people you put in charge to run my Power Point for sermons do a poor job.	The Power Point for my two sermons on Good Friday did not work and it impacted the quality of my preaching.
4. Taking care of the dog.	I am walking your dog each day while you go to work but this is no longer working for me in my retirement.
5. The condescending way you speak to and treat me after I hired you to build our stairs coming up to our front porch.	I hired you to build our stairs at a certain height and width. It's been done wrong twice by your employee and you're not taking responsibility for it.
6. You don't know what is happening in my life.	For the last four months our relationship has become increasingly lopsided. I call you each week to connect, but you no longer call me.

Note: Copies of a Ladder of Integrity Worksheet for you to use can be found on page 172. Two other examples of people using the Ladder can be found in Appendix E, pages 173-177.

Partner Activity (20 minutes/10 per person)

1. Find a neutral partner, a person with whom you do *not* have the issue, to practice going up the Ladder. Decide who will go first. Let your partner know who he/she is standing in for.
    - As the speaker:
        - Ask for permission.
        - Start at the bottom and go up the Ladder (see page 117).
        - Skip a sentence stem if it does not help you explore the issue.
        - Thank the listener when you're done.
    - As the listener:
        - Give the speaker your full attention.
        - Do not interrupt.
        - Thank the speaker for sharing when he/she is done.
2. Switch after ten minutes.

Small Group Sharing (10 minutes)

In groups of three or four:

1. What was the partner activity like for you? What did you learn?

2. What next step might you take to summarize the main points of your Ladder if you intend on sharing your value with the appropriate person?

3. How do you think this tool might better enable you to listen to God's voice?

▶ VIDEO: Closing Summary (5 minutes)

Video Notes

Remember: This skill is *not* for confronting someone, but for *getting clear within yourself.*

- When all blame has been removed, you are ready to talk to the other person.
- Many times we will use the Ladder, however, and realize we don't need now to go to the other person. Getting clear within ourselves will be enough.

Opportunities to use the Ladder of Integrity:

- Marriage (if there is goodwill between the spouses)
- Parenting
- Work (with your boss/colleagues)
- Church (leadership/staff/congregants)

It may take several times up the Ladder to "mine" your true value.

Jesus is our great example of integrity: "I have brought you [the Father] glory on earth by completing the work you gave me to do" (John 17:4).

Optional Session Wrap-up (5 minutes)

Together with your small group, ask any questions of clarification regarding this session and then briefly close in prayer.

PERSONAL ACTION STEPS

- Before the next session, write about a difficult issue, using the Ladder of Integrity to express your thoughts.
- After clarifying your value, decide if it is appropriate to share it with the person with whom you have the tension.

Between-Sessions Personal Study
Session Six

Read the pre-session assignment for Session 7 on pages 126–127. Use the space provided to note any insights or questions you might want to bring to the next group session.

Prayerfully read Week 6 of the *Emotionally Healthy Relationships Day by Day* devotional, "Climb the Ladder of Integrity." Use the space provided to answer the Questions to Consider and/or to journal your thoughts each day.

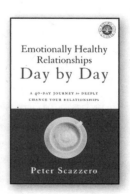

DAY 1 Questions to Consider:

Under what circumstance, or to whom, do you find it difficult to say no? Why?

What comes to mind when you consider where your "deep gladness" meets the world's "deep hunger"?

DAY 2 Questions to Consider:

Here are some signs that we are living a divided life, a life without integrity:

- We care too much what others think.
- We spin the truth, exaggerate, or lie to make ourselves look better.
- We blame others rather than taking responsibility for our words and actions.
- We avoid confrontation.
- We say yes when we prefer to say no.

Which of these characteristics, if any, might be true of you? What makes it difficult for you to live with integrity in this area of life?

How has God been seeking to get your attention lately? What is your "burning bush" equivalent—that issue that is burning but won't die?

DAY 3 Questions to Consider:

How might today be different if, instead of comparing your life to others or trying to avoid your "cup," you surrendered yourself to it?

In what areas of your life (values, attitudes, activities, lifestyle choices, etc.) might God be calling you to follow Daniel—to resist the values of the culture?

DAY 4 Questions to Consider:

As you consider taking off any "fig leaves" you may be wearing, how do you hear God's promises, "Do not fear. I love you. I will never leave you"?

In what areas of life do you sometimes feel indispensable? (For example, at home, at work, at church, in a friendship, with your extended family.) How might God be inviting you to let go?

DAY 5 Questions to Consider:

In which of your relationships might God be inviting you differentiate, to tolerate short-term discomfort for the sake of long-term growth—in you and in those around you?

Consider your interactions over the last twenty-four hours. In what ways, if any, did you choose your actions or words specifically to either gain approval or to avoid disapproval?

Fight Cleanly

Session Seven

PRE-SESSION READING

Most Christians we meet are poor at resolving conflict. There are at least two reasons for this: the first relates to wrong beliefs about peacemaking and the second relates to a lack of training and equipping in this area.

A tragically misinterpreted verse in the New Testament is Jesus' proclamation: "Blessed are the peacemakers, for they will be called sons of God" (Matthew 5:9). Most people think that Jesus calls us in this verse to be pacifiers and appeasers who ensure that nobody gets upset. We are to keep the peace, ignoring difficult issues and problems, making sure things remain stable and serene.

When, out of fear, we avoid conflict and appease people, we are false peacemakers. For example:

Karl is upset about the behavior of his spouse who constantly comes home late after work. He says nothing. Why? He thinks he is being like Christ by not saying anything, although he does give her a cold shoulder. He is a false peacemaker.

Pam disagrees with her coworkers at lunch when they slander her boss. She is afraid to speak up. She goes along. *I don't want to kill the atmosphere by speaking up and disagreeing,* she thinks. She is a false peacemaker.

Bob goes to dinner with ten other people. He is tight financially, so he orders only a salad and appetizer. Meanwhile, the other nine order appetizers, steak, wine, and desserts. When the bill comes, someone says, "Let's divide up the bill equally. It will take forever to figure it out." Everyone agrees. Bob is dying on the inside but won't say anything. He is a false peacemaker.

Yolanda is engaged. She would like more time to rethink her decision but is afraid that her fiancé and his family will get angry. She goes through with the wedding. She is a false peacemaker.

Ellen loves her parents. They are both quite critical about how she raises her children.

Each holiday is filled with tension. Ellen doesn't say anything because she doesn't want to hurt their feelings. She is a false peacemaker.

Sharon thinks her boyfriend is irresponsible but feels bad for him. *He has had so much pain already in his life*, she thinks. *How can I add to that?* So she backs down from telling him the truth about the way his behavior is slowly killing their relationship. The relationship dies a slow death. She is a false peacemaker.

The problem with all these scenarios is that the way of true peace will never come through pretending what is wrong is right! True peacemakers love God, others, and themselves enough to disrupt false peace. . . . You can't have the true peace of Christ's kingdom with lies and pretense. They must be exposed to the light and replaced with the truth. This is the mature, loving thing to do.

In the Beatitudes, Jesus explains to us the characteristics we need to display if we are to engage in true peacemaking—poverty of spirit, meekness, purity of heart, mercy, etc. (Matthew 5:3–11). He also follows the call to true peacemaking by stating that persecution will follow for those of us who follow him in this.

Nonetheless, unresolved conflicts are one of the greatest tensions in Christians' lives today. Most of us hate them. We don't know what to do with them. Instead of risking any more broken relationships, we prefer to ignore the difficult issues and settle for a "false peace," hoping against hope they will somehow go away. They don't. And we all learn, sooner or later, that you can't build Christ's kingdom on lies and pretense. Only the truth will do.

Many of us believe loving well is learned automatically, that it is just a "feeling." We underestimate the depth of our bad habits and what is needed to sustain long-term, Christlike change in our relationships.

This belief led us, over twenty-one years ago, to begin learning from a variety of sources, gathering and creating tools, to help us as followers of Jesus obey the command to love well. We wanted to move people from defensiveness, reactivity, and fear to openness, empathy, and vulnerability.

Teaching people to fight cleanly became one of the most important skills we learned.

—*Emotionally Healthy Spirituality*, Updated Edition, pages 175–178

GROUP MEETING

Daily Office (10 minutes)

Do one of the Daily Offices from Week 7 of *Emotionally Healthy Relationships Day by Day* to begin your session.

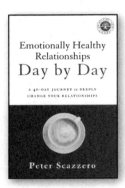

Introduction (2 minutes)

Most people are not very good at resolving conflicts.

When Jesus said, "Blessed are the peacemakers, for they will be called sons of God" (Matthew 5:9), most people think that Jesus calls us in this verse to be pacifiers and appeasers who ensure that nobody gets upset. We think he wants us to ignore difficult issues and problems, and make sure that things remain stable.

Yet conflict was central to the mission of Jesus. He disrupted the false peace of those all around him—the disciples, the crowds, the religious leaders, the Romans, and those buying and selling in the temple. He taught that true peacemaking disrupts false peace, even in families (see Matthew 10:34–36).

Why? You can't have the true peace of Christ's kingdom with lies and pretenses. True peace will never come through pretending that what is wrong is right. Lies must be exposed to the light and replaced with the truth. The real problem, however, is not in the conflict itself but in how we process and negotiate our differences.

Growing Connected (10 minutes)

1. *Day by Day* Debrief: We are hard-wired by God, not just for work and activity, but for stopping and resting in order to nurture our relationship with him. What are you

discovering about the importance of having a rhythm of stopping in order to be still and know that he is God (Psalm 46:10).

2. Turn to the person next to you and in a word or two describe how conflict typically was handled in your home growing up (e.g., avoidance, yelling, sarcasm, the silent treatment).

Bible Study (10 minutes)

After the fall of Jerusalem, Daniel, a young man at the time, was carried off to Babylon as a slave and placed in the king's "university" to be trained for leadership. Part of that training included a daily amount of food and wine from the king's table. Have a volunteer read aloud Daniel 1:8–17 below.

But Daniel resolved not to defile himself with the royal food and wine, and he asked the chief official for permission not to defile himself this way. Now God had caused the official to show favor and compassion to Daniel, but the official told Daniel, "I am afraid of my lord the king, who has assigned your food and drink. Why should he see you looking worse than the other young men your age? The king would then have my head because of you."

Daniel then said to the guard whom the chief official had appointed over Daniel, Hananiah, Mishael and Azariah, "Please test your servants for ten days: Give us nothing but vegetables to eat and water to drink. Then compare our appearance with that of the young men who eat the royal food, and treat your servants in accordance with what you see." So he agreed to this and tested them for ten days.

At the end of the ten days they looked healthier and better nourished than any of the young men who ate the royal food. So the guard took away their choice food and the wine they were to drink and gave them vegetables instead.

1. To these four young men God gave knowledge and understanding of all kinds of literature and learning. And Daniel could understand visions and dreams of all kinds. Consuming the royal food and wine was not permissible for Daniel. What steps did he take to resolve his conflict with those in authority over him?

2. Imagine yourself as Daniel. What might you have done?

3. Describe the result of Daniel's negotiation with the guard.

▶ VIDEO: Fight Cleanly (4 minutes)

Video Notes

A core discipleship issue for all followers in the new family of Jesus is to learn how to resolve conflicts maturely.

This skill builds on the previous skills taught in the *EH Relationships Course.*

The purpose: To resolve a conflict maturely by eliminating "dirty fighting" tactics, and by taking responsibility for a difficult issue.

Our families of origin have formed us to handle conflicts a certain way.

> e.g., "Don't get anyone upset."

> e.g., "Be nice."

> e.g., "Don't rock the boat."

Jesus' Model of True Peacemaking
- He brought disruption in order to bring true peace.
- He did not avoid conflict or appease people.
- He didn't ignore tensions or differences.

Key principle: True peace will never come by pretending that what is wrong is right.

⏸ *Pause the Video*

Workbook Activity (2 minutes)
Individual Activity (2 minutes)

Put a checkmark next to the dirty fighting tactics that apply to you.

DIRTY FIGHTING TACTICS[1]

☐ Silent treatment   ☐ Complaining   ☐ Anger/rage
☐ Lecturing   ☐ Denying   ☐ Passive-aggressive
☐ Blaming/attacking   ☐ Walking away   behavior
☐ Condescension   ☐ Placating   ☐ Lying
☐ Threatening gestures   ☐ Avoiding   ☐ Hitting/violence
☐ Name-calling   ☐ Shouting   ☐ Showing contempt
☐ Criticizing   ☐ Using "always"
☐ Sarcasm   and "never"

▶ *Resume Video* (11 minutes)

Video Notes
Fight Cleanly: The Wrong Way

Examples of two office workers and two roommates

Conflict resolution in the church is not very different from conflict resolution outside the church!

It's possible to be a Christian for five, fifteen, or even fifty years and still handle conflicts as if we were twelve years old in our family of origin.

A Clean Fight is about breaking negative generational patterns through the Spirit of God.

A Clean Fight is a negotiation between two people for the sake of the relationship.

Key principle: The person who asks for the Clean Fight is acknowledging he/she is the one with the issue.

Fight Cleanly: The Right Way
Jessica Models a Clean Fight with Her Mom

Steps to a Clean Fight
1. Ask permission. State the problem. "I notice . . ."

    e.g., "Mom, *I notice* that ever since I have moved back home from college, you regularly give me advice."

2. State why it is important to you. "I value . . ."

    e.g., "*I value* having an adult to adult relationship with you, rather than an adult-to-child relationship."

3. Fill in the following sentence: "When you . . . I feel . . ."

   e.g., "When *you* give me unsolicited advice, *I feel* hurt because I think that you don't think I'm responsible after having lived on my own for four years, graduated college, and now am working full-time."

4. State your request clearly, respectfully, specifically.

   e.g., "I'd like to ask that you refrain from giving me advice unless I ask for it."

5. Listener: Consider the request. In a few sentences, share your feelings and perspective.

   e.g., "Wow, Jessie, I had no idea how my words were affecting you. But as a mom, I have concerns and I see I can be overprotective at times."

   Listener: Say if you are willing to do all of it, some of it, or none of it.

   e.g., "I am willing to stop giving you advice. But once again, I am your mother and I might slip. I would like to ask you to gently remind me when I'm crossing your boundaries."

6. Speaker: Agree to the request or offer an alternative.

   e.g., "Mom, if you do slip and give me advice, how about if I signal you with the words *comprendé* or *gotcha* to let you know you have crossed a boundary."

   Listener responds.

   e.g., "That's great, Jessie."

7. Together, write your agreement and plan to review it in a few weeks.
   Speaker: My understanding of the agreement is:

   e.g., "Mom will refrain from giving me advice unless I ask for it. If she slips, I'll signal her with *comprendé* or *gotcha*."

   Listener: My understanding of the agreement is:

   e.g., "I won't give Jessie unsolicited advice, but if I slip, she will gently remind me by saying *comprendé* or *gotcha*."

8. Review the agreement in two to four weeks.

> e.g., "We will review the agreement on June 8 at 8:00 p.m."

⏸ *Pause the Video*

Workbook Activities (30 minutes)

Individual Activity (10 minutes)

Answer each of the four questions. Remember to stick to only one issue.

1. State the problem. "I notice . . ."

Be concrete when you state the problem. You must describe a behavior, not just the emotion. For example:
- "I notice you get frustrated with me when we're arguing," describes an emotion.
- "I notice you get up and walk away when we're arguing and you're frustrated with me," describes a behavior.

Other good examples:
- "I notice you call me after 11:00 p.m."
- "I notice you leave dirty dishes in the sink for more than a day."
- "I notice you leave your empty coffee cups in the car."
- "I notice you rarely fill the car up with gas."
- "I notice you don't answer my emails for at least a week."
- "I notice that you pick up your cell phone at least three times when we are together in a restaurant."
- I notice that I have to wait for you for at least ten minutes whenever I come to pick you up.

Pick a concrete behavior that is not a strong emotional issue for you.

2. State why it is important to you. "I value . . ."

3. Fill-in the following sentence: "When you _____,
   I feel _____."

4. State your request clearly, respectfully, and specifically, including details such as times and/or dates.

Partner Activity (20 minutes)

1. Find a partner. This is best done with the person with whom you have the issue. So, if it is possible now, partner with that person. Most of you, however, will be practicing with a neutral person. If that is the case, have your partner role-play.
2. Decide who will talk first, and then follow the process described below and on the next page.
3. After ten minutes, switch roles and repeat the process.

THE CLEAN FIGHT PROCESS

Speaker: Ask for permission to do a Clean Fight.

Listener: Remember to repeat back what you hear the speaker saying by paraphrasing after each sentence stem (steps 1–4).

Speaker:

1. State the problem. "I notice . . ."
2. State why it is important to you. "I value . . . because . . ."
3. Fill in the following sentence: "When you . . . I feel . . ."
4. State your request clearly, respectfully, and specifically, including details such as times and/or dates.

Listener:

    5. Consider the request. Briefly share your feelings and perspective on it.

    6. Are you willing to do all of it, part of it, or none of it?

Speaker:

    7. Agree on the (modified) request or offer an alternative. Keep going back and forth until you come to an agreement, but not more than three times.

Together:

    8. Write your agreement and make a plan to go over it in two to four weeks.

Speaker: My understanding of the agreement is:

Listener: My understanding of the agreement is:

Small Group Sharing (10 minutes)

In groups of three or four:

1. What was most helpful about the Clean Fight process? What was most difficult?

2. Jesus says: "Blessed are the peacemakers" (Matthew 5:9). What blessings might there be on the other side of learning this very important skill—in your personal life, relationships, work, or church?

▶ Closing Video (2 minutes)

Video Notes

Conflict is normal, important, and necessary if relationships are to enter their next level of growth and maturity.

Research shows 96 percent of arguments are determined in the first three minutes. Be careful how you start a conversation. (If you start off poorly, feel free to stop and say, "Hey, would you mind if we start again?")

If you find yourself stuck in a "fight" that is complex, speak to a mature mentor, pastor, or professional counselor.

Optional Session Wrap-up (5 minutes)

Together with your small group, ask any questions of clarification regarding this session and then briefly close in prayer.

PERSONAL ACTION STEPS

- During the next week, practice the Fight Cleanly skill around another issue, repeating the same process you learned in this session.

  I plan on practicing the Fight Cleanly skill:

  With whom? _____

  When? _____

- If you have time, read Appendix F, "The Emotionally Mature Christian," on page 178.

Between-Sessions Personal Study
Session Seven

Read the pre-session assignment for Session 8 on pages 144–145. Use the space provided to note any insights or questions you might want to bring to the next group session.

Prayerfully read Week 7 of the *Emotionally Healthy Relationships Day by Day* devotional, "Fight Cleanly." Use the space provided to answer the Questions to Consider and/or to journal your thoughts each day.

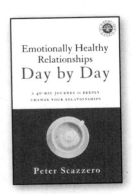

DAY 1 Questions to Consider:

In what kind of situations, or with whom, are you routinely tempted to avoid conflict and settle for a false peace?

If it's true that our enemies can be gifts-in-disguise from God, who in your life might be a "saint-maker"? In what way(s) might God be using this person to transform you?

DAY 2 Questions to Consider:

When was the last time God led you into a season of disorientation that ultimately resulted in a new orientation with fresh insights and growth?

In the last few days, what "small interruptions" have come into your life that offer an opportunity to practice choosing surrender?

DAY 3   Questions to Consider:

In what ways does God's simple promise, "I will be with you," give you courage to move toward your fears and toward reconciliation with someone with whom you have a conflict?

Who is someone that you suspect you may "have hurt, diminished, or dismissed, intentionally or carelessly"? What might God's invitation be when you consider the question, "What am I going to do about it?"

DAY 4   Questions to Consider:

Jesus said, "I desire mercy, not sacrifice" (Matthew 9:13). What is one concrete way you can show mercy to someone today?

What might it look like for you to respond to criticism in the nondefensive, humble way John the Short did?

DAY 5 Questions to Consider:

In what situation, and with whom, are you tempted to "cut off someone's ear," to defend yourself, or something you love, by acting in ways that are not truly loving?

As you consider a person who has hurt you, what words or phrases from the Compassion Prayer impact you most?

Develop a "Rule of Life" to Implement Emotionally Healthy Skills

Session Eight

PRE-SESSION READING

Please don't be intimidated by the word *rule*. The word comes from the Greek for "trellis." A trellis is a tool that enables a grapevine to get off the ground and grow upward, becoming more fruitful and productive. In the same way, a Rule of Life is a trellis that helps us abide in Christ and become more fruitful spiritually.[1]

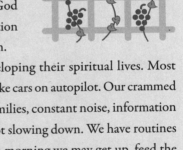

A Rule of Life, very simply, is an intentional, conscious plan to keep God at the center of everything we do. It provides guidelines to help us continually remember God as the Source of our lives. It includes our unique combination of spiritual practices that provide structure and direction for us to intentionally pay attention and remember God in everything we do. The starting point and foundation of any Rule is a desire to be with God and to love him.

Very few people have a conscious plan for developing their spiritual lives. Most Christians are not intentional, but rather functional, like cars on autopilot. Our crammed schedules, endless to-do lists, demanding jobs and families, constant noise, information bombardment, and anxieties keep us speeding up, not slowing down. We have routines to manage other parts of our lives. For example, each morning we may get up, feed the cat, then make coffee, exercise, get dressed for work, and eat breakfast.

The reality, however, is that every person has an unconscious Rule for developing his or her spiritual life. We each have our values and ways of doing things. This may include, for example, attending a church on Sundays, participating in a small group, serving in a ministry, and/or ten minutes for prayer and Bible reading before going to bed.

However, our present spiritual practices are not enough to keep us afloat in the ocean of the beast, the Babylon of our twenty-first-century world. Fighting against such a strong current, without the anchor of a Rule of Life, is almost impossible. Eventually we find ourselves unfocused, distracted, and adrift spiritually.

Is it any wonder that most people live off other people's spirituality rather than taking the time to develop their own direct experience of God? Most Christians talk about prayer but don't pray. Most believe the Bible as the Word of God but have little idea what it says. Our goals for our children differ little from those of "pagans" who do not know God. Like the world, we, too, grade people based on their education, wealth, beauty, and popularity.

Nurturing a growing spirituality with depth in our present-day culture will require a thoughtful, conscious, intentional plan for our spiritual lives. To plan well, however, requires we go back to Daniel and early church history to consider the roots of this hidden treasure.

Nebuchadnezzar and his Babylonian armies, with their gods, conquered Jerusalem and carried off most of the city's inhabitants as slaves. One of those was a young teenager named Daniel. Cut off from his family, teachers, friends, food, culture, and language, Daniel was brought into the Babylonian court of the king and sent to the best university in the land. He studied a completely foreign and pagan way of viewing the world—history, mathematics, medicine, religion, literature. He learned about myths, astrology, sorcery, and magic—all things banned in Israel. Pagan priests and counselors educated him in their wisdom and religion. In Babylon's effort to assimilate Daniel, they even changed his name.

Babylon had one simple goal: to eliminate Daniel's distinctiveness as a God follower and absorb him into the values of their culture.

How did Daniel resist the enormous power of Babylon? He was not a cloistered monk living behind walls. He had heavy job responsibilities with people giving him orders. He had a minimal support system, and, I imagine, a very long to-do list each day.

What Daniel did have was a plan, a Rule of Life. He did not leave the development of his interior life to chance. He knew "going to church on Sundays, along with a fifteen-minute daily quiet time" would never be enough. He knew what he was up against. While we know little of the specifics, it is clear that he oriented his entire life around loving God. He renounced certain activities, such as eating the king's contaminated food (Daniel 1) and engaged in others, such as the Daily Office (Daniel 6). Daniel somehow fed himself spiritually and blossomed into an extraordinary man of God in this hostile environment. He knew resisting the beast of Babylon and thriving required a plan that would enable him to pay attention to God.

—*Emotionally Healthy Spirituality*, Updated Edition, pages190–192

GROUP MEETING

Daily Office (10 minutes)

Do one of the Daily Offices from Week 8 of *Emotionally Healthy Relationships Day by Day* to begin your session.

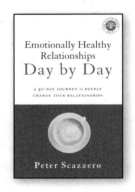

Introduction (2 minutes)

Ordering our lives so that we are intentionally paying attention to God, and remembering him in all we do, is no small task. Our crammed schedules, endless to-do lists, demanding jobs and families, noisy surroundings, and anxieties keep us from actually making the changes we desire.

We often find ourselves unfocused, distracted, and spiritually adrift.

Nurturing a growing spirituality in which we love God and others well calls for a conscious, purposeful plan. To implement what we have learned in this course, and reverse decades of unhealthy ways of living, requires thoughtfulness. To help us do this, we will uncover an ancient, buried church treasure called the "Rule of Life."

Growing Connected (10 minutes)

1. *Day by Day* Debrief: The goal of stopping for the Daily Office is to increase our awareness of God's presence throughout the entire day—in the midst of our activities. In what new ways, small or large, are you beginning to experience this greater awareness of God during the day as you practice the Daily Office?

2. Turn to the person next to you and share which of the last seven sessions has impacted you the most. Briefly explain.

Bible Study (15 minutes)

Have a volunteer read aloud Luke 14:25–30 below and then discuss the questions that follow.

> Large crowds were traveling with Jesus, and turning to them he said: "If anyone comes to me and does not hate father and mother, wife and children, brothers and sisters—yes, even their own life—such a person cannot be my disciple. And whoever does not carry their cross and follow me cannot be my disciple. Suppose one of you wants to build a tower. Won't you first sit down and estimate the cost to see if you have enough money to complete it? For if you lay the foundation and are not able to finish it, everyone who sees it will ridicule you, saying, 'This person began to build and wasn't able to finish.'"

1. The word *hate* is a common Hebrew exaggeration used to make a point. In what sense is Jesus asking us to "hate" our family and even our own life?

2. When a person carried a cross in first-century Palestine, this meant they were about to be executed. In this light, what do you think might be the implications for you to "carry [your] cross" and die, especially as it relates to implementing these new skills you have learned in this *EH Relationships Course*?

3. How does Jesus' story of the person building a tower illustrate the challenge before us in making long-lasting changes in our lives?

 **VIDEO: Develop a "Rule of Life" to Implement Emotionally Healthy Relationship Skills** (5 minutes)

Video Notes

Introduction

the emotionally healthy
DISCIPLESHIP COURSE

A discipleship model proven to deeply change people's lives

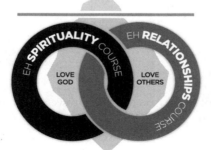

Part 1: Emotionally Healthy Spirituality

Learn to LOVE GOD

1. The Problem of Emotionally Unhealthy Spirituality
2. Know Yourself That You May Know God
3. Going Back in Order to Go Forward
4. Journey through the Wall
5. Enlarge Your Soul through Grief and Loss
6. Discover the Rhythms of the Daily Office and Sabbath
7. Grow into an Emotionally Healthy Adult
8. Go to the Next Step to Develop a "Rule of Life"

Part 2: Emotionally Healthy Relationships

Learn to LOVE OTHERS

1. Check Your Community Temperature Reading
2. Stop Mind Reading and Clarify Expectations
3. Genogram Your Family
4. Explore the Iceberg
5. Listen Incarnationally
6. Climb the Ladder to Integrity
7. Fight Cleanly
8. Develop a "Rule of Life" to Implement Your New Learnings

EH SPIRITUALITY COURSE · EH RELATIONSHIPS COURSE

LOVE GOD · LOVE OTHERS

Learn more: **emotionallyhealthy.org**

"By this all will know that you are my disciples, if you love one another." (John 13:35)

The purpose: The goal of this session is to create a specific plan to implement the Emotionally Healthy Relationship Skills into your life in order to transform your relationship with God, yourself, and others.

EMOTIONALLY HEALTHY **SKILLS SUMMARY**

THE SKILL	ITS PURPOSE	USE IT WITH	WHEN TO USE IT
1. Community Temperature Reading	To increase awareness within yourself of your God-given value and to build healthy relationships with others	Spouse, children, extended family members, peers (in the classroom or workplace)	In groups of two or more—in formal settings and informal settings (5–30 minutes)
2. Stop Mind Reading	To clarify what another person is thinking instead of making assumptions	Anyone you think is making assumptions of you and anyone of whom you might be making assumptions	Anywhere, anytime, any setting (1–3 minutes)
3. Clarify Expectations	To recognize whether certain expectations are valid or not, and to clarify them with others	With anyone — friends, coworkers, schoolmates, employees, family	One-on-one with another person, or as a group (5–20 minutes)
4. Genogram Your Family	To become aware of, and break, unhealthy, sinful patterns in your family of origin to fulfill your God-given purpose	Alone or with a trusted friend, spouse, or mentor	By yourself or one-on-one (10–45 minutes)
5. Explore the Iceberg	To become aware of your emotions with the goal of processing them and discerning God's will	Alone or out loud with another person	By yourself (in your journal) or out loud with another person asking you the sentence stems (5–20 minutes)
6. Listen Incarnationally	To listen at a heart level with empathy, attuned to the words and nonverbal cues of another person (i.e., the other person feels felt by you)	Spouse, family members, close friends, colleagues, or significant others	Set aside a specific, uninterrupted time. (5–20 minutes)

| 7. Climb the Ladder of Integrity | To clarify your values by processing your thoughts and feelings (and, if appropriate, to assert yourself respectfully) | Anyone—friend, spouse, coworker—you have tension with and know fairly well | Begin by yourself (in your journal) or with a neutral person. It takes time to mine those core values that are important to you. (15–45 minutes) |
| 8. Fight Cleanly | To resolve a conflict maturely by: 1) eliminating dirty fighting tactics 2) taking responsibility for a difficult issue | Everyone—friends, spouse, coworkers, fellow church members, family members | Starting out, do this with one other person. Once you've mastered this skill, you can then begin using it in other settings. (45–70 minutes) |

Create a Rule of Life

- A Rule of Life is like a trellis, a structure to help you grow and mature, bear fruit for Christ.
- It is an intentional, conscious plan to apply the *EH Relationships Course* in all your relationships as a disciple in the new family of Jesus.

 *Pause the Video*

Workbook Activities (20 minutes)

Individual Activity: Develop a "Rule of Life" (10 minutes)

As you craft your Rule of Life, consider the diagram on the next page.

We were created to receive and give the love of God. The EH Relationships Skills are hands-on tools that help us receive and give this love in very practical ways.

As you reflect on the eight Emotionally Healthy Relationships Skills from this Course, thoughtfully consider the following questions:

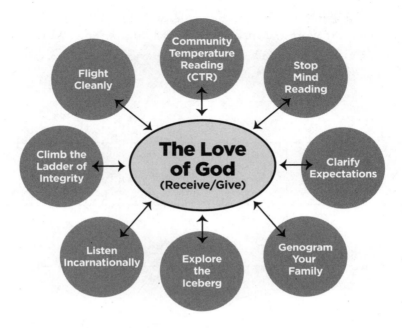

Which skill(s) have you found most helpful?

What positive impact are you experiencing now in your life and/or relationships as a result of using these skills?

Which relationships skill(s) might God be inviting you to intentionally focus on during the next three months? Write it/them down in the chart below. Note: We recommend that you start with only one to three skills. When you experience some success, then you can move on to other skills.

Skill	Who Will You Use It With?	How Often (Daily, Weekly, Monthly)?

What obstacles come to mind when you think of implementing these skills into your life? What obstacles or problems might you face if you *don't* implement them?

What one or two steps could you take to overcome the obstacles you just identified?

Partner Activity (5 minutes)

Share your chart from the Individual Activity with one other person.

▶ Closing Video (3 minutes)

Video Notes

Regardless of your race, culture, country of origin, family, age, or context (urban, suburban, or rural), implementing these skills is countercultural.

These skills clash with how we commonly relate to God, ourselves, and other people.

Persevere patiently. The important thing is progress.

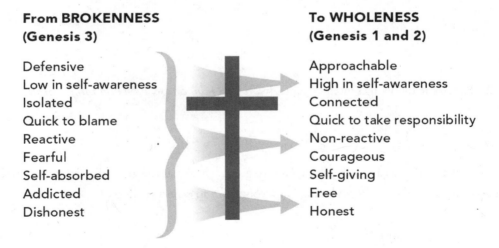

RELATIONSHIPS IN THE NEW FAMILY OF JESUS

From BROKENNESS (Genesis 3)	To WHOLENESS (Genesis 1 and 2)
Defensive	Approachable
Low in self-awareness	High in self-awareness
Isolated	Connected
Quick to blame	Quick to take responsibility
Reactive	Non-reactive
Fearful	Courageous
Self-absorbed	Self-giving
Addicted	Free
Dishonest	Honest

"You are the salt of the earth. But if the salt loses its saltiness, how can it be made salty again? . . . You are the light of the world. A town built on a hill cannot be hidden . . . In the same way, let your light shine before others, that they may see your good deeds and glorify your Father in heaven." (Matthew 5:13–14, 16)

We exist to be a gift and blessing to the world. We do this first and foremost by loving others.

Our hope and prayer—you will bring these EH Relationships Skills to your workplace, school, family, and neighborhood for Jesus' sake.

Final Group Time (25 minutes)

Stay together as a Table Group and share your answers to the following questions.

1. What is one hope or dream you have as you go forward with these skills?

2. Finish the following sentence stem: *As a result of this course, I am beginning to realize . . .*

Pray together as a group, asking God to give each of you the grace to sustain the small steps you have taken to begin loving God, yourself, and others well.

Personal Study for the Coming Days

Session Eight

We encouraged you to take the Personal EHS Assessment before you began *The EH Relationships Course* to get a sense of whether you were an emotional infant, child, adolescent, or adult. Now we invite you take the Personal EHS Assessment once again after having completed the course.

Remember: We grow slowly chronologically. We also grow slowly spiritually. Give God thanks for any progress you may have made over the last two to three months. All is a gift of grace.

Note: This assessment can also be taken free online or downloaded as a PDF at www .emotionallyhealthy.org/.

*   *   *

Prayerfully read Week 8 of the *Emotionally Healthy Relationships Day by Day* devotional, "Develop a 'Rule of Life' to Implement Emotionally Healthy Skills." Use the space provided to answer the Questions to Consider and/or to journal your thoughts each day.

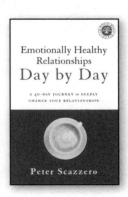

DAY 1 Questions to Consider:

Briefly reflect on your relationships with a few people you routinely interact with. What "harsh and dreadful things" might love require of you in these relationships?

Moses commits an act of rebellion when he disregards God's instructions. He still does God's work, but from a place of frustration and on his own terms. In what ways, if any, do you recognize this pattern in your own life?

DAY 2 Questions to Consider:

How do you respond to the truth that your life is *taken*, *blessed*, *broken*, and *given*? Which of these four words speaks most to you today?

What unhealthy pattern or "dragon skin" do you most desire for God to free you from right now?

DAY 3 Questions to Consider:

What is one small way you can take initiative today to serve Christ by loving those around you?

God said to Julian, "All will be well, and all will be well, and every kind of thing will be well." In what relationship or circumstance in your own life do you most need to receive this promise from God?

DAY 4 Questions to Consider:

How might you be a true spiritual friend to someone in your life this week?

How might you create additional space in your life for silence today?

DAY 5 Questions to Consider:

Speak to God about your willingness—or unwillingness—to follow his sealed orders, wherever they may lead you. What joys or fears are you aware of?

In what one area of your life might God be inviting you to patiently trust him today?

Leader's Guide

The EH Relationships Course has been designed and structured to offer a high-quality teaching experience in a large group setting while at the same time offering close community support within a table small group.

Why?

We realized that this content was so critical that it needed to be offered in a centralized format that would ensure a high-quality experience for participants.

First, we wanted every newcomer and member to grasp our core elements of following Jesus in a way that deeply transforms us. And, secondly, we wanted to ensure the long-term integration of EHS into every aspect of the church. The radical, introductory call of discipleship found in the *EH Relationships Course* serves as both an entry point and an essential bridge into the larger EHS vision. For this reason, the *EH Relationships Course* is offered at least one or two times a year in churches (along with the *EH Spirituality Course*).

The EH Spirituality Course equips us in a discipleship paradigm that deeply changes **our relationship with God**. *The EH Relationships Course* then deeply changes **our relationship with others**. Perhaps most important to note is that these deep changes in our relationship with God and others happen because of the profound transformation happening **in us**. For this reason, the two Courses together form the foundation of a powerful discipleship strategy.

At New Life Fellowship Church our discipleship strategy builds on these two Courses. Go to www.emotionallyhealthy.org to download a variety of excellent, free resources to help you serve as the Point Leader or a Small Group Table Leader.

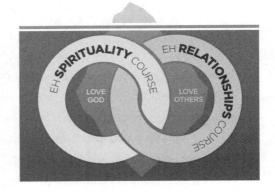

General Guidelines

1. Be sure to work through the workbook content before each session. Becoming familiar with the material and instructions will allow you to comfortably lead your group. If possible, we highly recommend you watch the video segments as well.

2. The Point Leader, or another appointed person, will need to select a Daily Office to open each session. The initial large-group Daily Office (for Session 1) is particularly challenging because it will be the first exposure to silence and stillness for many people. Have them turn to the appropriate page in the *EH Relationships Day by Day* book and explain to them the elements of the Office before you begin. Refer to the Silence and Stillness guidelines below or display them on a PowerPoint slide as a brief orientation. While the Office may be difficult for some people, it will set a tone for the Course's centrality on being with Jesus. Specific suggestions on how to lead these Offices each week, and what you might say each week as an introduction, can be found at www.emotionallyhealthy.org/.

SILENCE & STILLNESS GUIDELINES

The Lord will fight for you; you need only to be still. Ex 14:14

- Sit down and take a few deep breaths to settle into the silence.

- Choose a very simple prayer to express your openness and desire for God.
  (e.g. Abba, Father, Holy Spirit, Jesus, Here I am Lord)

- Close your eyes and offer this prayer to Jesus, allowing His will and love full access in your life.

- When you become distracted, offer again your simple prayer back to God.

---

3. Have extra copies of this workbook and the *Emotionally Healthy Relationships Day by Day* devotional available for each participant to purchase at the first two sessions. Make scholarships available, if possible, for those who need financial assistance.

4. Each session—a combination of doing a Daily Office together, the video presentation and discussion, group and individual activities—will require 90–120 minutes to complete. Respect everyone by beginning and ending on time.

5. Set up the meeting room in a way that will comfortably seat all participants, preferably at a table so that everyone can see each other. Arrive at least fifteen minutes ahead of time to greet group members individually as they come in.

6. The nature of this material easily lends itself to lengthy sharing. One of your greatest challenges as the Small Group Table Leader will be to keep the group focused and to share within the time frames allotted for each part of the session. Remember that each of these sessions could easily have been expanded into its own course. We have kept them together to serve a biblical framework that serves as an introduction into a life with God that goes beyond "tip of the iceberg spirituality." The implementation of these truths will involve the rest of people's lives.

7. If your table small group is large, we encourage you to break into smaller groups of three to four people so that everyone has a chance to participate.

8. When appropriate, it will be helpful if you lead by example—being vulnerable and open with life examples from your own journey. Remember, we are only experts on *our own* journey.

9. Respect where each person is in their journey with Christ. The Holy Spirit will prompt and lead each person differently and at different paces through this material. Remember that people change slowly—that includes you!

10. Being with Jesus is the core of *The EH Relationships Course*. Learning the practice of silence to listen and *be with God* two or three times a day is the core discipline leading to a deep personal transformation. You will want to be sure to faithfully meet with God each day in the silence and stillness using *Emotionally Healthy Relationships Day by Day: A 40 Day Journey with the Daily Office* and encourage participants to do the same.

    Beginning in Session 2, the following question is asked in the "Growing Connected" section: What obstacles, difficulties, or successes did you experience with God this week using the *EH Relationships Day by Day* devotional? It is important that you also share your struggles, failures, and learnings.

Additional Suggestions[1]

1. Avoid answering your own questions. Feel free to rephrase a question.
2. Encourage more than one answer to each question. Ask, "What do the rest of you think?" or "Anyone else?"

3. Try to be affirming whenever possible. Let people know you appreciate their contributions.

4. Try not to reject an answer. If it is clearly wrong, ask, "What in the passage led you to that conclusion?"

5. Avoid going off on tangents. If people wander off course, gently bring them back to the subject at hand.

Specific Guidelines for Each Session

SESSION ONE: Introduction and Take Your Community Temperature Reading

Before the Session:

- Be sure to watch Pete's brief training video for Table Small Group leaders at www .emotionallyhealthy.org/ for an overview of the progression of the eight sessions and other helps.

During the Session:

- Keep topics and examples light whenever possible. The goal of this Course is to teach skills that you will practice for a lifetime. Therefore, it is always best to begin with topics and examples that are not too provocative or volatile. These skills, once mastered, can serve to solve more difficult, challenging issues.

- Note that the position of each item on the Community Temperature Reading thermometer does not denote its importance. Each area is important.

- People sometimes ask, "What is the difference between a puzzle and a complaint?" *Puzzles* are used to keep us from negative interpretations when we don't have all the facts. *Complaints* assume that all the data is before us and that we have a possible solution. At times, a single issue can be in both categories. For example, Pete said he would be home by 6:00 p.m. If he arrives at 6:45 p.m., Geri can say, "I'm puzzled, Pete, because you are home so late." She can also make it a complaint/solution, "I notice that you said you'd be home by 6:00 p.m., and it is 6:45 p.m. I'd prefer it if you called me when you are going to be late."

- We've included optional wrap-up time at the end of every session. Use this time to field any questions of clarification that group members may have and to remind them of Action Step items and the Between-Sessions Personal Study. Then briefly close in prayer.

SESSION TWO: *Stop Mind Reading and Clarify Expectations*

During the Session:

- During the individual activity for Clarify Expectations, it will be important to emphasize the word *simple*. The goal here is to practice with the simple things before moving to the more complex. You will want to give one or two examples (e.g., who does the dishes, puts out the garbage, returns phone calls, or locks the front door). Topics may include issues related to parenting, roommates, holidays, vacations, money, family members, church, neighbors, work, friends, or household chores/responsibilities.

- People sometimes ask, "What is the difference between sharing a complaint and clarifying an expectation?" Each skill is used in the context of how it originates in your own mind. Let's take the issue of Geri realizing there was an expectation that she cook seven nights a week. Sharing her complaint ("I notice . . . I prefer . . .") as part of a Community Temperature Reading (CTR) wasn't enough. She realized this particular issue involved uncovering an unspoken, unconscious, and un-agreed upon expectation with Pete. This needed the time, space, and language appropriate for the Clarify Expectations skill. Many issues can be resolved by simply clarifying the expectations around them. Others, however, require negotiation to resolve. This will be covered in Session 7: "Fight Cleanly." Clarify Expectations is a skill for clarifying assumptions and determining if your expectations are valid or invalid. A Clean Fight helps to negotiate and resolve an issue.

SESSION THREE: *Genogram Your Family*

Before the Session:

- Be sure to preview the video for Session 3, following along in the workbook. Because of the nature of this session, it is very important for you to get a feel for the content, exercises, and flow of each section. This session, unlike the others, requires diagramming and labeling. Moreover, there are three transitions in and out of the video.

- Have extra copies of a larger Genogram worksheet (page 65) that people could use. This can be downloaded at www.emotionallyhealthy.org/. It is also helpful to provide pencils with erasers so they can easily make changes to their genograms.

During the Session:

- People will work at different paces in filling out their genograms. You will want to keep them aware of the time frame. It is highly unlikely that people will finish in the time allotted. Remember, the primary goal for this session is awareness. Please make sure that everyone answers question 4 (individual activity, page 66) before time runs out.

- This session may be emotionally difficult for some people. Remind the group that we all come from flawed families due to the sin in our world. Our goal is to raise awareness and begin making one or two changes in the sinful patterns from our past that hinder our growth in Christ.

- We ask that everyone does their genogram through the eyes of their childhood, between eight and twelve years old, because these are such formative, significant years for most of us.

- Looking back into our families of origin is one very helpful way to clarify who God has uniquely made us to be as adults. We are better able to appreciate the gifts and positive legacies that have been deposited into us and to differentiate from our family members as appropriate. The term *differentiation* refers to a person's capacity to "define his or her own life's goals and values apart from the pressures of those around him or her." The pre-session reading for Climb the Ladder of Integrity in Session 6 explains differentiation more fully.

SESSION FOUR: *Explore the Iceberg*

During the Session:

- You may want to read "Discovering God's Will and Your Emotions" in *Emotionally Healthy Spirituality*, Updated Edition (pages 48–49) for a brief summary on the role of feelings in discerning God's will.

- As noted in the instructions for the individual activity on pages 82–83, you as Point Leader will read aloud the four questions, allowing two minutes for each response. At the one-and-a-half-minute mark for "What are you angry about?" ask, "If there was one more thing you were angry about, what would it be?" Also, at the one-and-a-half-minute mark for "What are you sad about?" ask, "If there was one more thing you were sad about, what would it be?" We have found that this helps many people.

- This exercise may bring up significant pain for some members of the group—such as unresolved anger, sadness that has not been grieved, or shame that has been masked.

Remember that this is a limited exercise with one goal—to help people begin to become aware of how much is going on inside of them. This is not the time to fix anyone or give advice. Giving people space to express their feelings is gift enough in this setting.

SESSION FIVE: Listen Incarnationally

During the Session:

- Encourage any two people you notice not facing each other during the exercise to do so. When we face each other we are more aware of the verbal and nonverbal communications going on.

SESSION SIX: Climb the Ladder of Integrity

During the Session:

- Bible Study: What did Paul risk in confronting Peter? Peter was the head of the church in Jerusalem and one of the original twelve apostles. Paul was not. By publicly confronting Peter for his hypocrisy, Paul risked being slandered and misunderstood. Yet if Paul had chosen to be silent, he would have violated his own integrity with regard to the truth of the gospel. Moreover, this would have introduced a legalism into the church at Antioch that would have had far-reaching, divisive implications.
- Notice the star next to number seven on the Ladder of Integrity (page 117). Clarifying one's value is at the heart of this tool. At times, a deeper value lies beneath the initial value. For example, Pete was not simply clarifying the value of attending his nephew's wedding. Beneath that was a value of family connection and relationship, especially with his older brother Anthony.

SESSION SEVEN: Fight Cleanly

During the Session:

- During the partner activity, emphasize that the listener should repeat/paraphrase the speaker's words during steps 1–4.
- The purpose of step 2 ("I value . . . because . . .") is to help people pause to think more deeply about why the issue is important to them. We want them to share from a stance of values rather than a stance of right or wrong.

- For step 3 ("When you ... I feel ..."), you may want to refer the group to Appendix C (page 171) for a list of feeling words. People often jump to thoughts and opinions instead of feelings.
- If there is time at the end of the study, read aloud Appendix F, "The Emotionally Mature Christian" (page 178).
- For group members desiring professional or pastoral counseling, use any of the following language: *When you are looking to find a professional or pastoral counselor, begin by asking your pastor or church leaders. If you want to use a counselor in the network of your insurance coverage, we recommend that you identify a provider who specializes in the issue you want to address (e.g., marriage, depression, anger, grief, anxiety, or addictions). Call a few counselors with that specialty and interview them. Ask them questions such as: "How do you handle this issue with other people? How much experience do you have in this area?" Pick someone with whom you feel comfortable.*

SESSION EIGHT: Develop a Rule of Life to Implement Emotionally Healthy Skills

During the Session:

- It is *very* important to leave twenty minutes for sharing during the Final Group Time at the end of this session (questions 1 and 2). Be sure to pace the group so there is sufficient time for people to share. For this session, do not divide the group unless it contains more than twelve people. The benefit of listening to what people have learned during the course is priceless.

APPENDICES

Appendix A

Sample Family Genogram

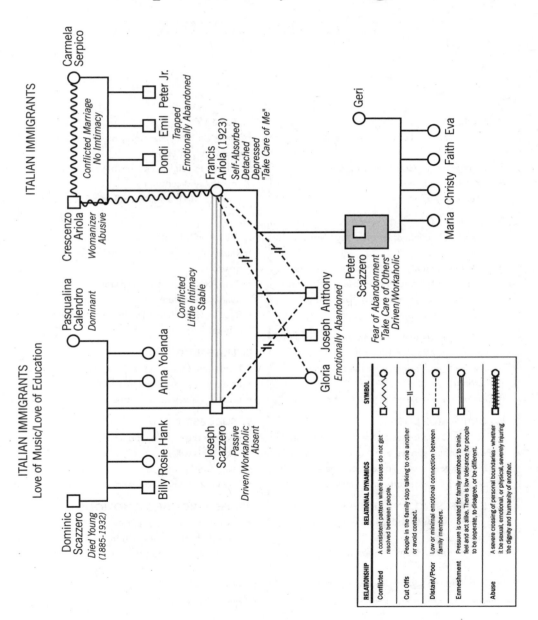

Appendix B

Biblical Family Commandments

1. MONEY
- You are a steward of God's money. It belongs to him.
- Be generous, as God enables you.
- Live within your means and do not go into unnecessary debt.

2. CONFLICT
- Do not avoid conflict; learn to negotiate differences.
- Allow God to mature you through conflicts.
- Eliminate dirty fighting tactics (e.g., blaming, passive-aggressiveness, appeasement).

3. SEX
- Receive your sexuality, maleness or femaleness, as a beautiful gift from God.
- Reserve sexual intimacy for the covenant of marriage.
- Do not use people or let yourself be used.

4. GRIEF AND LOSS
- Your griefs and losses are important to God.
- Pay attention and wait on him in your losses.
- Grieving your losses, instead of ignoring them, leads to maturity and compassion.

5. EXPRESSING ANGER
- Explore the hurts and fears behind your anger.
- Do not stuff or project anger; use it to assert yourself.
- Do not let the sun go down on your anger.

6. FAMILY
- Thank God for sovereignly placing you in your family of origin.
- Unlearn the sinful patterns of your family, country, and culture.
- Learn to "do life" differently in the family of Jesus.

7. RELATIONSHIPS
- Repair ruptured relationships as much as possible.
- Respect each person's individuality for healthy togetherness.
- Receive God's love in order to give love to others.

8. LISTENING
- Listen to explore and to understand.
- Be slow to speak and quick to listen.
- Listen as a way to love others.

9. SUCCESS
- Become the person God intended you to be, and do his will.
- Learn from your failures.
- Live in brokenness, depending upon God.

10. FEELINGS AND EMOTIONS
- Pay attention to your emotions.
- Prayerfully and carefully think about your feelings before you act on them.
- Experience your emotions in order to love others well.

Appendix C

Feeling Words

Afraid

Anxious
Desperate
Fearful
Helpless
Nervous
Pressured
Shocked
Terrified
Worried

Angry

Annoyed
Bitter
Defensive
Frustrated
Furious
Humiliated
Offended
Resentful

Hurt

Abandoned
Cheated
Crushed
Defeated
Deserted
Heartbroken
Lonely
Misunderstood
Upset

Sad

Ashamed
Depressed
Disappointed
Discouraged
Disillusioned
Hopeless
Miserable
Moody

Doubtful

Confused
Distrustful
Hesitant
Indecisive
Puzzled
Skeptical
Uncertain

Interested

Amazed
Challenged
Concerned
Curious
Eager
Enthusiastic
Excited
Inspired

Loving

Appreciative
Compassionate
Honored
Sympathetic
Tender

Happy

Comfortable
Contented
Grateful
Hopeful
Joyful
Lighthearted
Peaceful
Pleased
Relaxed

Physical

Aware
Awkward
Empty
Exhausted
Refreshed
Repulsed
Strong
Tense
Weak

Miscellaneous

Bold
Bored
Cooperative
Determined
Distant
Impatient
Indifferent
Jealous

LADDER OF INTEGRITY **WORKSHEET**

12. I hope and look forward to...

11. I think my honest sharing will benefit our relationship by...

10. The most important thing I want you to know is...

9. One thing I could do to improve the situation is...

8. I am willing/not willing to...

7. This issue is important to me because I value... and I violate that value when...

6. What my reaction tells me about me is...

5. My feelings about this are...

4. My need in this issue is...

3. My part in this is...

2. I'm anxious in talking about this because...

1. Right now the issue on my mind is...

Appendix E

Sample Ladders of Integrity

Sample #1

Julie, a newly hired administrative assistant, did this Ladder with Linda, a member of the pastoral staff.

1. Right now the issue on my mind is . . .

. . . how I perceived an email you sent to me on my second day of work. I barely knew you, and you emailed a two-sentence request for me to make you a flyer. It felt curt to me because there was very little information given, without discussing it in person to let me know what your ministry is about and to establish a sense of clarity of expectations in working together. The message that I told myself was that you are only interested in the work that I can produce for you, and you don't see me as a person or as a new staff team member.

2. I'm anxious about talking about this because . . .

. . . I'm used to avoiding problems by distancing myself from people who I feel have offended me. I grew up with the message that you have to prove that you're not at fault, and that you're good enough. I'm scared to find out what you will say or think about the matter because it may reveal more about my own flaws and faulty thinking.

3. My part in this is . . .

. . . I came into this new work environment with a set of assumptions on how the staff would approach me and that my first week on the job would be focused on getting oriented and trained. Instead of speaking up to communicate what I was thinking and to request that I take a week to get oriented, I simply became offended by my faulty assumptions.

4. My need in this issue is . . .

. . . to let you know how important building rapport is with those that I work with, that is, a face-to-face personable contact—at least initially when we don't know one another at all. I need to know that I am valued as a person and not just for the work that I produce. I also need to hear from you about your experience of that interaction.

5. My feelings about this are . . .

Fear . . . I am scared because I'm not used to addressing tension with people I don't know very well and with whom have not had the chance to build a sense of trust. But I'm also feeling more open now that I have taken the time to reflect on the situation—and I am curious to hear your perspective.

6. What my reaction tells me about me is . . .

My fear tells me why I have been avoiding the issue and distancing myself from you. My gradual openness tells me that I am moving away from avoidance and letting go of the resentment.

7. This issue is important to me because I value . . .

I value working in an environment where there is rapport among coworkers. Since we will be working together, it is important to me that efforts are made to establish rapport, especially when someone is new to the team. I also value clear expectations of my work responsibilities because I didn't think your request was part of my job expectations when I was hired.

. . . and I violate that value when . . .

. . . I don't initiate rapport with others out of a reaction that thinks they are not making efforts to build rapport with me. I also violated my value of having unclear expectations, making my own assumptions about things and not speaking up enough to clarify expectations.

8. I am willing to . . .

I am willing to try to gain your perspective. I am also willing to accept that others may not value building rapport in the workplace as much as I do.

I am not willing to . . .

. . . work in a place where there is no sense of rapport with those I'm supporting (some context of being acquainted with each other that goes beyond only the work that I can produce for you).

9. One thing I could do to improve the situation is . . .

. . . look for clarity because my initial way of dealing with it wasn't helpful. I really needed to find out your perspective. Also, I could declare myself in a healthy and respectful way, make known my limits and priorities, get clarity on my job description, and be more specific.

10. The most important thing I want you to know is . . .

I've come to realize how important it is to me to have rapport with people that I work with.

11. I think my honest sharing will benefit our relationship by . . .

. . . creating more understanding between us, letting you know what I value rather than making faulty assumptions that you should know what is important to me. Also, learning what you value will help me to understand how I can best work with you.

12. I hope and look forward to . . .

I hope I can hear from you and what you value in the workplace environment. I look forward to working together with this newfound sense of mutual understanding.

• • •

Sample #2

Rich, a teaching pastor, did this Ladder with Peter, the person responsible for the technical aspects of the service.

1. Right now the issue on my mind is . . .

. . . the frustration that happens with PowerPoint during my sermons, but in particular the fiasco with the PowerPoint support during my sermon for our two Good Friday services.

2. I'm anxious in talking about this because . . .

. . . I'm afraid that if I express my annoyance and if I'm honest about my feelings, you might think less of me.

3. My part in this is . . .

. . . I haven't been clear with you in emphasizing how important this is for me. In addition, I've shared my thoughts in passing with you, but I haven't said anything about how I feel.

4. My need in this is . . .

. . . I need to know that you know that this is really important to me.

5. My feelings about his are...

annoyance, frustration, anxiety and fear that it will happen again.

6. What my reaction tells me about me is . . .

. . . I really care about what people think about me and, as a result, to keep people liking me, I don't typically declare my needs and feelings.

7. This issue is important to me because I value . . .

. . . the privilege and incredible opportunity to partner with God in forming people through preaching. I also value the connection that I have with our community because these are opportunities I'll never get back. And when there is not adequate technical support to communicate effectively, it's challenging for me to remain focused. I also value our friendship and want to be honest with you regarding my feelings.

8. I am willing to . . .

. . . hear your thoughts on this, and willing to talk about ways to improve media support.

I'm not willing to . . .

. . . pretend that this isn't really significant to me.

9. One thing I could do to improve the situation is . . .

. . . to share my feelings and thoughts clearly and directly with you, and to give you an opportunity to share your perspective and feelings as well.

10. The most important thing I want you to know is . . .

. . . that I really value the opportunities I get to share God's Word with our church, and when I work hard to communicate effectively and don't get the kind of tech/media support necessary to do so, it's very frustrating.

11. I think my honest sharing will benefit our relationship by . . .

. . . my taking responsibility to communicate with you clearly and not assuming that you know what I value. I won't be resentful and unfairly hold against you the fact that you don't know what I value.

12. I hope and look forward to . . .

. . . being able to have the privilege to partner with God in the forming process of our church as well as continuing to clarify expectations to bring this matter to a good resolution. I also hope to have a follow-up conversation to hear your thoughts/feelings and what our next steps are.

The Emotionally Mature Christian

1. I am deeply convinced that I am loved by Christ, so I don't inappropriately borrow that love from others.
2. I love my neighbor as I love myself—embracing my singleness as I bond with others or, in marriage, giving first priority to my spouse (and children).
3. I am able to leave my family of origin and function as an inner-directed, separate adult.
4. I am deeply in tune with my own emotions and feelings.
5. I am able to listen with empathy without having to fix, change, or save others.
6. I can speak clearly, honestly, and respectfully on my own behalf.
7. I can express my anger, hurt, or fear without blaming, appeasing, or holding grudges.
8. I value my own dignity as a human being made in God's image through self-respect and self-care.
9. I walk in community while respecting each person's uniqueness.
10. I can receive criticism without becoming defensive.
11. I can state my own beliefs and values without becoming adversarial.
12. I live in truth, not pretense, spin, illusions, or exaggerations.
13. I embrace my limits as a gift.
14. I am able to negotiate, respect, and celebrate differences.
15. I am willing to initiate and repair relationships (as much as it is possible) when they have been ruptured.

Appendix G

Receive and Give God's Love through Skills

Take Your Community Temperature Reading

- You *receive* the love of God through the joy of self-expression.
- You *give* the love of God by being present to others as they reveal themselves.

Stop Mind Reading and Clarify Expectations

- You *receive* the love of God through the freedom that comes with speaking the truth.
- You *give* the love of God by not "bearing false witness against your neighbor."

Genogram Your Family

- You *receive* the love of God through positive family legacies and the healing of family wounds.
- You *give* the love of God by changing sinful patterns and offering forgiveness to others.

Explore the Iceberg

- You *receive* the love of God through the gift of emotions as they guide and protect you.
- You *give* the love of God by sharing your feelings and owning them so they are not projected onto others in unhealthy ways.

Listen Incarnationally

- You *receive* the love of God by entering the world of another human being through deep listening, receiving a gift through giving a gift.
- You *give* the love of God by being a safe presence for another person. You are saying, "Your life counts."

Climb the Ladder of Integrity

- You *receive* the love of God by being true to your God-given life and integrity.
- You *give* the love of God by being honest and not blaming or projecting.

Fight Cleanly

- You *receive* the love of God through respecting your own wants and needs.
- You *give* the love of God by taking the initiative to maturely resolve differences for the sake of your relationships.

Notes

Session 1: Take Your Community Temperature Reading (CTR)

1. I am grateful to Lori Gordon, the founder of the PAIRS program, for the concept of emotional infants, children, adolescents, and adults; see Lori Gordon with John Fandson, *Passage to Intimacy* (self-published; rev. version 2000), 181–191.
2. This concept is explained more fully in Chapter 7, "Grow into an Emotionally Mature Adult," of *Emotionally Healthy Spirituality*, Updated Edition (Grand Rapids: Zondervan, 2017).
3. We learned this very helpful phrase from Lori Gordon and the PAIRS Foundation (www .pairs.com) in their adaptation of the Community Temperature Reading, which was originally developed by Virginia Satir.

Session 2: Stop Mind Reading and Clarify Expectations

1. Every time I make an assumption about someone who has hurt or disappointed me without confirming it, I believe a lie about this person in my head. This assumption is a misrepresentation of reality. Because I have not checked it out with the other person, it is very possible that I am believing something untrue. It is also likely that I will pass that false assumption around to others. When we leave reality for a mental creation of our own doing (hidden assumptions), we create a counterfeit world. When we do this, it can be said that we exclude God from our lives because God does not exist outside of reality and truth. In doing so, we wreck relationships by creating endless confusion and conflict. . . . The Bible has much to say about not taking on the role of judge to others (see Matthew 7:1–5). (See *Emotionally Healthy Spirituality*, Updated Edition, pages 181–182.)

Session 3: Genogram Your Family

1. See Judith Rich Harris, *The Nurture Assumption: Why Children Turn Out the Way They Do* (New York: Touchstone, 1998). The "nurture" proponents argue that what children learn in early years about relationships and rules for living life sets the pattern for the rest of their lives. The "nature" proponents look at genetic factors and biology. Judith Harris has argued that it is neither. Rather, she states that our peer groups of childhood and adolescence shape our behavior and attitudes for life.
2. See Rodney Clapp, *Families at the Crossroads: Beyond Traditional and Modern Options* (Downers Grove, IL: InterVarsity Press, 1993) and Ray Anderson and Dennis Guernsey, *On Being Family: A Social Theology of the Family* (Grand Rapids: Eerdmans, 1985), 158.

3. For a full theological treatment of this session, read Chapter 6, "Break the Power of the Past," in *The Emotionally Healthy Church* (Zondervan, 2010) and Chapter 3, "Go Back in Order to Go Forward," in *Emotionally Healthy Spirituality*, Updated Edition. It is common to observe certain patterns from one generation to the next, such as divorce, alcoholism, addictive behavior, sexual abuse, poor marriages, a child running away, mistrust of authority, pregnancy out of wedlock, an inability to sustain stable relationships, etc. Scientists and sociologists have been debating for decades whether this is a result of "nature" (i.e., our DNA) or "nurture" (i.e., our environment), or both. The Bible doesn't answer this question. It only states that this is a mysterious law of God's universe.

Session 4: Explore the Iceberg

1. Daniel Goleman, *Emotional Intelligence: Why It Can Matter More Than IQ* (New York: Bantam, 1995); idem, *Working with Emotional Intelligence* (New York: Bantam, 1998); idem, *Primal Leadership: Realizing the Power of Emotional Intelligence* (Cambridge, MA: Harvard Business School Press, 2002).

2. See www.brainyquote.com/quotes/quotes/b/q133380.html.

3. For a full discussion of biblical material related to this topic, go to Chapter 3, "Discipleship's Next Frontier—Emotional Health," and Chapter 9, "Embracing Grief and Loss," in *The Emotionally Healthy Church* (Zondervan, 2010). Pages 69–73 of *Emotionally Healthy Spirituality*, Updated Edition (Zondervan, 2017) include a helpful section on how God feels in Scripture and how we feel—even if we are not aware of it. *The Emotionally Healthy Woman* also has an excellent chapter entitled "Quit Denying Anger, Sadness, and Fear."

Session 5: Listen Incarnationally

1. Quoted in Brennan Manning, *Abba's Child: The Cry of the Heart for Intimate Belonging* (Colorado Springs: NavPress, 1994), 29–30.

Session 6: Climb the Ladder of Integrity

1. I am using the words *true self* in a way similar to M. Robert Mulholland Jr. In footnote 1 of chapter 2 in *The Deeper Journey*, Mulholland states: "Self is used here not in the contemporary sense of the psychological 'self,' an implicitly reductionistic term, but in the larger biblical sense of personhood framed within the context of a life lived in relationship with God, in community with others and as part of creation."

2. Michael Kerr and Murray Bowen, *Family Evaluation: The Role of the Family as an Emotional Unit That Governs Individual Behavior and Development* (New York: Norton Press, 1988), 97–109.

Session 7: Fight Cleanly

1. We first learned an adaptation of this from the Pairs Foundation (www.pairs.com).

Session 8: Develop a "Rule of Life" to Implement Emotionally Healthy Skills

1. Jane Tomaine, *St. Benedict's Toolbox: The Nuts and Bolts of Everyday Benedictine Living* (Harrisburg, PA: Morehouse Publishing, 2005), 5.

Leader's Guide

1. Adapted from James F. Nyquist and Jack Kuhatschek, *Leading Bible Discussions* (Downers Grove, Ill.: InterVarsity Press, 1985).

About the Authors

Geri Scazzero is the author of the bestselling *The Emotionally Healthy Woman*, *The Emotionally Healthy Woman Workbook*, and coauthor of *The Emotionally Healthy Relationships Course*. She is also, along with her husband Pete, the cofounder of Emotionally Healthy Spirituality, equipping the church in a discipleship that deeply changes lives.

Geri has served on staff at New Life Fellowship Church in New York City for the last twenty-nine years and is a popular speaker to pastors, church leaders, and at women's conferences—both in North America and internationally.

Connect with Geri on Facebook (**www.facebook.com/GeriScazzero**).

Pete Scazzero, along with his wife, Geri, are the founders of Emotionally Healthy Discipleship, a ground-breaking ministry that moves the church forward by slowing the church down, in order to multiply deeply changed leaders and disciples. This journey began when Pete founded New Life Fellowship Church in Queens, New York, a large, multiracial church with more than seventy-three countries represented—where he served as the senior pastor for twenty-six years.

Pete hosts the top ranked Emotionally Healthy Leader podcast and is the author of a number of bestselling books, including *The Emotionally Healthy Leader* and *Emotionally Healthy Spirituality*. He is also the author of *The Emotionally Healthy Discipleship Course* (Part 1 and 2) that has transformed tens of thousands of lives around the world. For more information, visit emotionallyhealthy.org or connect with Pete on Twitter, Facebook, or Instagram @petescazzero.

For more information, visit emotionallyhealthy.org.

The Emotionally Healthy
DISCIPLESHIP COURSE:
Part 1 & 2

Congratulations on completing *Emotionally Healthy Relationships: Part 2*

Now What?!

It's time to begin *Emotionally Healthy Spirituality: Part 1*

COURSE CONTENT INCLUDES:

Session 1: The Problem of Emotionally Unhealthy Spirituality
Session 2: Know Yourself That You May Know God
Session 3: Going Back in Order to Go Forward
Session 4: Journey through the Wall
Session 5: Enlarge Your Soul through Grief and Loss
Session 6: Discover the Rhythms of the Daily Office and Sabbath
Session 7: Grow into an Emotionally Healthy Adult
Session 8: Go to the Next Step to Develop a "Rule of Life"

Get started at **emotionallyhealthy.org/lead**

Leader's Resource Vault

to equip you to lead
The Emotionally Healthy
Discipleship Course:
Part 1 & 2

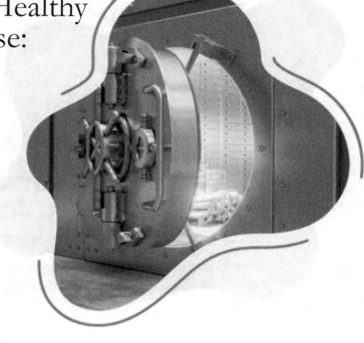

Free exclusive content includes:

- **Level 1 Training:** Mastering the Launch of the Emotionally Healthy Discipleship Course (Videos/Handouts)
- **Level 2 Training:** Mastering the Transformation of Your Entire Church Culture (Videos/Handouts)
- Planning Timelines, Session Schedules
- Access to a Certified EH Discipleship Course Coach
- Invitation to Join Private Facebook Group with Point Leaders from around the World
- Promotional Graphics/Certificates of Completion for Participants

Get access today at **emotionallyhealthy.org/vault**

Over 2 million downloads annually in 120+ countries.

THE EMOTIONALLY HEALTHY LEADER PODCAST
with Pete Scazzero

 Start listening now at **emotionallyhealthy.org/podcast**

 ZONDERVAN®

Go Deeper with Emotionally Healthy Discipleship

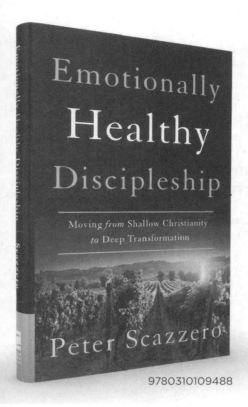

9780310109488

Part 1: The Current State of Discipleship
- The Four Failures that Undermine Deep Discipleship
- The Emotionally Healthy Discipleship Personal Assessment

Part 2: The Seven Marks of Healthy Discipleship
- Be Before You Do
- Follow the Crucified, Not the Americanized, Jesus
- Embrace God's Gift of Limits
- Discover the Treasures Buried in Grief and Loss
- Make Love the Measure of Maturity
- Break the Power of the Past
- Lead Out of Weakness and Vulnerability

Find out more at **emotionallyhealthy.org/discipleship**

Purchase the Book • Download a Free Discussion Guide and Videos

 emotionally
HEALTHY DISCIPLESHIP

 ZONDERVAN®

Are you an Emotional Infant, Child, Teen or Adult?

Take the Personal Assessment

This powerful 15-minute diagnostic tool enables you to determine your level of maturity.

This tool was created to help individuals, teams, or churches get a sense of whether their discipleship has touched the emotional components of their lives and, if so, how much. Each stage of emotional maturity is described fully at the end of the assessment.

Take the assessment at **emotionallyhealthy.org/mature**

How Emotionally Healthy Are You?

CHECKLIST | EMOTIONALLY HEALTHY **RELATIONSHIPS** COURSE

SESSION #	WORKBOOK	VIDEO (or live)	DAY-BY-DAY
1. Intro & Community Temperature Reading (CTR)	☐ Read Introduction ☐ Fill out Session 1	☐ Watch Session 1	☐ Prayerfully read Intro & Week 1
2. Stop Mind Reading and Clarify Expectations	☐ Read Introduction ☐ Fill out Session 2	☐ Watch Session 2	☐ Prayerfully read Week 2
3. Genogram Your Family	☐ Read Introduction ☐ Fill out Session 3	☐ Watch Session 3	☐ Prayerfully read Week 3
4. Explore the Iceberg	☐ Read Introduction ☐ Fill out Session 4	☐ Watch Session 4	☐ Prayerfully read Week 4
5. Incarnational Listening	☐ Read Introduction ☐ Fill out Session 5	☐ Watch Session 5	☐ Prayerfully read Week 5
6. Climb the Ladder of Integrity	☐ Read Introduction ☐ Fill out Session 6	☐ Watch Session 6	☐ Prayerfully read Week 6
7. Clean Fighting	☐ Read Introduction ☐ Fill out Session 7	☐ Watch Session 7	☐ Prayerfully read Week 7
8. Develop a "Rule of Life" Plan	☐ Read Introduction ☐ Fill out Session 8	☐ Watch Session 8	☐ Prayerfully read Week 8

Congratulations on completing **The Emotionally Healthy (EH) Relationships Course**, the second half of The EH Discipleship Courses.

Go to *emotionallyhealthy.org* to receive your **Certificate of Completion.**